Legally Yours

First Edition	2013
Reprint	**2017**

Legally Yours

Justice V.R. Krishna Iyer
Former Judge, Supreme Court of India

Universal Law Publishing
an imprint of LexisNexis

LexisNexis®

This book is a publication of **LexisNexis**
(A Division of RELX India Pvt Ltd)
14th floor, Building No 10, Tower–B, DLF Cyber City, Phase-II,
Gurgaon–122002, Haryana, India.
Tel : + 91 124 4774444 Fax: + 91 124 4774100
Website : www.lexisnexis.co.in / E-mail : help.in@lexisnexis.com

Justice V.R. Krishna Iyer, *Legally Yours,* First Edition, Reprint 2017

ISBN: 978-93-5035-262-5

Printed by: Sanat Printers, Haryana

Printed and bound in India.

CONTENTS

Then (1958) and Now (2012)

1. When I came to the Bar in 1958, I applied for membership and was refused mainly because I was Home Minister in a Communist Government and so assumed to be violent. Later from the same Bar I was chosen to be a judge of the High Court and the Bar on my leaving for Delhi passed resolution of tribute as one of the finest judges.
2. Free legal aid to the needy and the weak was virtually unknown when I came in 1958. But in later years a legal aid pattern where every poor person could claim free legal services was made a reality. Bail was rare in the primitive days of 1958. But with my progressive liberalization bail was the rule and jails the exemption. Parole was strict in 1958 but was very liberal in the later years. Death sentence was *de facto* abolished in the later years although was common in the late 50's. Public Interest Litigation was rare when I came into the Bar but became frequent and democratic in the later years. Thanks to my judgment and of some of my colleagues.
3. Prisoners had no activities like sports or voice in the cooking and management of the prisons. But my liberalization of prisons gave access to prisoners to visit exhibitions have gains and a democratic voice in the management of these institutions.
4. When I came to the High Court the judges worked for 200 days in a year with huge arrears. I made them work for 10 days more. Though they resisted first—under my pressure they yielded to it.
5. I was detained in custody for a day in the police station as a detainee to the surprise of many and later in jail for a month. My father moved the then Chief Minister in Madras. Since there was no ground worthwhile I was released from further

detention in jail. This was a unique experience in my life and was a new chapter in the history of Kerala prisons.

6. Prisoners were not paid wages for work done and had to work free. I introduced the system of work and wage which lend them dignity. One of the prisoners a musical artist went to sing in the AIR and his remuneration sent to his wife who was otherwise starving. This gesture enabled her to live a descent life. Prisoners were allowed to continue their studies and even take examinations by my policy of promoting development even while in prison. This was a humanist measure I introduced.

7. Even while a lawyer I was President of the District Education Council and in that capacity I was sued for a huge sum of money as damages caused by neglect. I moved the Government that I cannot be held liable as there was no case of neglect. Sir Alladi Krishnaswamy Iyer was the Advocate General of the Government. He advised the Government that there was no case to hold me liable and the case was withdrawn. This too was an unusual event for a member of the bar to suffer and that too, at the threshold in ones career.

Judicial Appointments and Disappointments

The Constitution of India operates through in happy harmony with the instrumentalities of the Executive and the Legislature. But the Judiciary exercising democratic power to be truly great must enjoy independence of a high order. But independence became dangerous and undemocratic unless there is a constitutional discipline with rules of good conduct and accountability sans which the robes may prove arrogant. It is in this context Chief Justice Kapadia's recent observations have to be reconciled with what the Law Minister Salman Khurshid has observed about judicial propriety. It is this reconciliation of the trinity of instrumentality in their functionalism that does justice to the Constitution at work. A great and grand chapter on judicial sublime behaviour to forbid the 'robes' becoming unruly or rude but ever sober is obligatory. A la! the recent conflict of *Ipse Dixit* between Chief Justice S.H. Kapadia and Law Minister Salman Khurshid.

Chief Justice S.H. Kapadia's observations at an event at the Supreme Court of India on Independence Day underlining the need for the government to balance judicial accountability with judicial independence, possibly alluding to the Judicial Standards and Accountability Bill pending before Parliament, has once again put the focus on certain crucial issues confronting the polity.

The Constitution of India has three instrumentalities — Executive, Legislative and Judicative. The implementation of the State's laws and policies is the responsibility of the Executive. The Cabinet headed by the Prime Minister at the Centre and the Cabinet led by the Chief Minister in the States, are its principal agencies. The rule of law governs the administration.

Parliament consisting of two Houses and Legislatures at the State level make law. When the Executive and the Legislature do anything that is arbitrary, or contrary to the constitutional provisions, the Judiciary has the power to correct them by issuing directions under article 143. The Constitution lays down the fundamental rights, and if the States do not safeguard them, any citizen can approach the Supreme Court for the issue of a writ to defend his or her fundamental rights.

Thus, among the three instrumentalities the Judiciary has pre-eminence. But the Judiciary itself has to act according to the Constitution and work within the framework of the Constitution.

Felix Frankfurter aptly pointed out thus: "Judges as persons, or courts as institutions, are entitled to no greater immunity from criticism than other persons or institutions. Just because the holders of judicial office are identified with the interests of justice they may forget their common human frailties and fallibilities. There have sometimes been martinets upon the Bench as there have also been pompous wielders of authority who have used the paraphernalia of power in support of what they called their dignity. Therefore judges must be kept mindful of their limitations and of their ultimate public responsibility by a vigorous stream of criticism expressed with candor however blunt."

Judges are the ultimate authority in the interpretation of the Constitution, and so must be learned in the law and in the cultural wealth of the world. This was emphasised by Justice Learned Hand thus: "I venture to believe that it is as important to a judge called upon to pass on a question of constitutional law, to have at least a bowing acquaintance with Acton and Maitland, with Thucydides, Gibbon and Carlyle, with Homer, Dante, Shakespeare and Milton, with Machiavelli, Montaigne and Rabelais, with Plato, Bacon, Hume and Kant, as with the books which have been specifically written on the subject. For in such matters everything turns upon the spirit in which he approaches the questions before him. The words he must construe are empty vessels into which he can pour nearly anything he will. Men do not gather figs of thistles, nor supply institutions from judges whose outlook is limited by parish or class. They must be aware that there are before them more than verbal problems; more than final solutions cast in generalizations of universal applicability. They must be aware of the changing social tensions in every society which make it an organism; which demand new schemata of adaptation; which will disrupt it, if rigidly confined."

The point I seek to make is with respect to the supreme position of the judges and the vital role they play in the working of the Constitution and the laws. But, how judges are being appointed is a matter of concern. Simply put, the President appoints them, but in this the President only carries out the Cabinet's decisions.

The Preamble to the Constitution lays down as the fundamentals of the paramount law that India shall be a socialist, secular democratic Republic which shall enforce justice — social, economic and political — and ensure liberty of thought, expression, belief, faith and worship, equality of status and of opportunity, and promote among them fraternity, ensuring the individual's dignity and the nation's unity and integrity.

But who will select the judges, and ascertain their qualifications and class character? Unless there is a clear statement of the principles of selection, the required character and conduct of judges in a democracy may fail since they will often belong to a class of the proprietariat, and the proletariat will have no voice in the governance: the proprietariat will remain the ruling class.

Winston Churchill made this position clear with respect to Britain thus: "The courts hold justly a high, and I think, unequalled pre-eminence in the respect of the world in criminal cases, and in civil cases between man and man, no doubt, they deserve and command the respect and admiration of all classes of the community, but where class issues are involved, it is impossible to pretend that the courts command the same degree of general confidence. On the contrary, they do not, and a very large number of our population have been led to the opinion that they are, unconsciously, no doubt, biased.

Lord Scrutton asked: "Where are your impartial Judges? They all move in the same circle as the employers, and they are all educated and nursed in the same ideas as the employers. How can a labour man or a trade unionist get impartial justice? It is very difficult sometimes to be sure that you have put yourself into a thoroughly impartial position between two disputants, one of your own class and one not of your class."

We in India have under the Constitution the same weaknesses pointed out by Churchill, with the result that socialism and social justice remain a promise on paper. Then came a new creation called collegiums. The concept was brought in by a narrow majority of one in a 5-4 decision of the Supreme Court for the selection of judges. It was binding on the Executive, the decisions of which in turn were bound to be implemented by the President.

Thus, today we have a curious creation with no backing under the Constitution, except a ruling of the Supreme Court, and that too taken based a very thin majority in a single ruling. Today, the collegium on its own makes the selection. There is no structure to hear the public in the process of selection. No principle is laid down, no investigation is made, and a sort of anarchy prevails.

In a minimal sense, the selection of judges of the highest Court is done in an unprincipled manner, without investigation or study of the class character by the members of the collegium. There has been criticism of the judges so selected, but the collegium is not answerable to anyone.

In these circumstances, the Union Law Minister has stated that the government proposes to change the collegium system and substitute it with a Commission. But, how should the Commission be constituted? To whom will it be answerable? What are the guiding principles to be followed by the Commission? These issues remain to be publicly discussed. A constitutional amendment, with a special chapter of the Judiciary, is needed. Such an amendment can come about only through Parliamentary action.

Surely a Commission to select judges for the Supreme Court has to be of high standing. It must be of the highest order, of a status equal to that of the Prime Minister or a Supreme Court Judge. The Commission's Chairman should be the Chief Justice of India.

In the process of selection, an investigation into the character, class bias, communal leanings and any other imputations that members of the public may make, may have to be investigated. This has to be done not by the police, which function under the government, but by an independent secret investigation agency functioning under the Commission's control. These and other views expressed by outstanding critics may have to be considered.

The Commission has to be totally independent and its ideology should be broadly in accord with the values of the Constitution. It should naturally uphold the sovereignty of the Constitution beyond pressures from political parties and powerful corporations, and be prepared to act without fear or favour, affection or ill-will. It should act independently — such should be its composition and operation. The Commission should be immune to legal proceedings, civil and criminal. It should be removed only by a High Tribunal consisting of the Chief Justice of India and the Chief Justice of all the High Courts sitting together and deciding on any charges publicly made. We, the People of India, should have a free expression in the Commission's process.

Kapadia Contra Khurshid

If the Constitution is to function without chaos and in comity, the Independence of the judiciary stressed by the Chief Justice Kapadia and the overbearing tampering with the basic policies of the Executive have to be reconciled and respected. This reconciliation or mutual nexus is fundamental or else the Legislature will impeach the judges out of office and the judiciary will jail the Legislatures for contempt. So the high values enshrined in the judicial independence and the effective and fearless implementation of sound policies by the Executive subject to the constitutional provision shall both operate freely and fearlessly.

Independence of the Judiciary is not arbitrary exercise without principles and regulation, but it is under constitutional control focused in the welfare and liberty of the people. Independence is fundamental and supreme. But it is not the personal privilege or special luxury of the judges. This immunity is integral part of the fundamental right of the citizen. He has an unrestricted access to move the court if he has a grievance. This is independent of executive or other authority. This freedom of the citizen seeking redress forensic is totally independent and only if the court is absolutely free from fear and independent he can function with judicial autonomy. Thus, Independence of the Judiciary is basically for the citizen's freedom to seek and secure his justice. This explains why judicial independence in a democracy is also the independence of the citizen to insist from the robed brethren the right to demand and secure justice under the law and be accountable to him under the law. Thus the judge is vested with Independence more as a facility to fulfill his professional functionalism to impart justice without fear of favour, affection or ill-will. Independence and accountability are not conceptually contradictory but complimentary dimensions of the same power shared by the judge as the giver and the Indian citizen as the seeker. The Chief Justice, who speaks with dignity, taciturnity and wisely is wholly right. If you truncate his independence you diminish his trustee power to give fearless justice to the smallest citizen who can challenge the overbearing authority of the richer Big Business so long as he has supreme independent courts which is accountable to the citizen. No judge shall be liable to civil or criminal action without the sanction of the Chief Justice who is the guardian of judicial immunity. The robe is not an arbitrary or irresponsible attire but accountable to the free people of *Swaraj*. India committed to the great freedoms and duties that make our culture truly pan-Indian. It is time to make this paramount position a constitutional mandate penetratingly perceived. We discover an integral nexus and a natural bond between Judicial Independence and Accountability – who is supreme? Not the Executive who have to obey the Legislature who decides the functional ordinance of the Legislature. The voter though he be rich or small, worker or employer, the proletariat or proprietariat – in short 'We, the People of India'. "The little man, walking into a little booth, with a little pencil, making a little cross on a little bit of paper – no amount of rhetoric or voluminous discussion can possibly diminish the overwhelming importance of the point." (Winston Churchill). The judge in his public or private capacity has to behave sublimely. A grand Code of Conduct of the Judiciary high and low has been drawn up by former Chief Justice Verma and his colleague of Supreme Court in an unanimous paper is set out below as adopted by Full Bench of Supreme Court on 7th May, 1997.

1. Justice must not merely be done but it must also be seen to be done. The behaviour and conduct of members of the higher Judiciary must reaffirm the people's faith in the impartiality of the Judiciary. Accordingly any act of the Judge of the Supreme Court or a High Court, whether in official or personal capacity, which erodes the credibility of this perception has to be avoided.

2. A Judge should not contest the election to any office of a club, society or other association; further he shall not hold such elective office except in a society or association connected with the law.

3. Close association with individual members of the Bar, particularly those who practice in the same court, shall be eschewed.

4. A judge shall not permit any member of his immediate family, such as spouse, son, daughter, son-in-law or daughter-in-law or any other close relative, if a member of the Bar, to appear before him or even be associated in any manner with a cause to be dealt with by him.
5. No member of his family, who is a member of the Bar, shall be permitted to use the residence in which the Judge actually resides or other facilities for professional work.
6. A Judge should practise a degree of aloofness consistent with the dignity of his office.
7. A Judge shall not hear and decide a matter in which a member of his family, a close relation or a friend is concerned.
8. A Judge shall not enter into public debate or express his views in public on political matters that are pending or are likely to arise for judicial determination.
9. A Judge is expected to let his judgments speak for themselves. He shall not give interview to the media.
10. A Judge shall not accept gifts or hospitality except from his family, close relations and friends.
11. A Judge shall not hear and decide a matter in a company in which he holds shares is concerned unless he has disclosed his interest and no objection to his hearing and deciding the matter is raised.
12. A Judge shall not speculate in shares, stocks or the like.
13. A Judge shall not engage directly or indirectly in trade or business, either by himself or in association with any other person. (Publication of a legal treatise or any activity in the nature of a hobby shall not be construed as a trade or business).
14. A Judge should not ask for, accept contributions or otherwise actively associate himself with the raising of any fund for any purpose.
15. A Judge should not seek any financial benefit in the form of a perquisite or privilege attached to his office unless it is clearly available. Any doubt in this behalf must be got resolved and clarified through the Chief Justice.

16. Every Judge must at all times be conscious that he is under the public gauze and there should be no act or omission by him which is unbecoming of the high office he occupies and the public esteem in which that office is held.

Justice is a constitutional obligation and mandatory in its operation. It has to be transparent and never secret. A judge is the finest citizen and his life public and private must be above board. "Suspicion is the *upas* tree under whose shade reason fails and justice dies" (Ingersoll) Justices must be above suspicion and must resign from office if there is a dark shade in their life. This is the price Judges pay for holding their high office which marks the noblest sector of society. They shall not be too rich in a society of indigents nor too arrogant or pompous on the Bench. In other words they should be of good behaviour according to the guidelines evolved by the Judges themselves during the term of Chief Justice J.S. Verma. The higher judiciaries are a higher class of citizens, transparent and committed to fraternity and peace. They shall be secular and never be involved in altercation. On the Bench they must display the virtue spelt out by Socrates: "Four things belong to a judge: to hear courteously, to answer wisely, to consider soberly and to decide impartially".

Let me wind up with what I once wrote:

> "On the whole, constitutional jurisprudence although in print socialist, has capriciously been interpreted to the prejudice of the weaker sections notwithstanding article 46 and Part IV of the Constitution (Fundamental Duties). Judges are not above the law nor are they final or infallible. The Parliament has the constituent power to undo contra-constitutional rulings, as Indira Gandhi did in the nationalisation of banks and the abolition of privy purses and F.D. Roosevelt did when he threatened to pack the Supreme Court in the USA. Nehru in the first amendment to the Constitution warned that the Supreme Court is not the Third Chamber of the Parliament. The 'tryst with destiny' that Nehru explained in his historic speech is still miles away because the appointment of judges with reference to their social philosophy, it would appear, is not a criterion by the collegium".

Morning Miscellany

Every dawn I first finish the routine which ends up with a hot cup of coffee. Then I begin with Shiva who is the divine power of well-being of your unnecessary self-intend the well-being of all creative animate and inanimate. So give priority to a worshipful turn inside the temple. It is a good walk free from the menace of traffic and mundane thought and devoted to divine values. The first thing I do every day is to read the striking central news in the Mathrubhoomi and the Manorama. Today it was the resignation of Mamata, a bold lady, who stood for the people in demanding withdrawal of the price hike of diesel, a blow on the poor and their Right to Life. In modern dignified way of life which is a fundamental right you have to have a hired vehicle. Diesel is the fuel mostly in use and the price hike means common man's freedom of movement is curtailed which means his freedom of association, communication and the very right to life itself is prejudiced. A Government under the Constitution whatever its compulsions cannot invade the most fundamental rights of the citizen, the right to life itself. In this sense a Government which makes life a difficult process is unconstitutional. In this sense Mamata is justified in her withdrawal of support from the Central Government. But Parliament is stultified when it is a matter of members and we find in this case some other party because Mulayam Singh has been roped in as stop gap support. This is unscrupulous when a party till now alien suddenly jumps in not because of conviction but because of opportunism. Mulayam may demand anything and the precarious position of the Central Government will be a dependencia syndrome. For a great country like Bharat it cannot command international respect if it has no stable Government with its own democratic manifesto. I pity the Prime Minister who is otherwise a man of integrity has to depend on a non-entity. Virtually India will be ruled not by majority party in Parliament but by a small man and a small party governing the governing party. The nation and the democratic Republic lose their stature and the great tryst with destiny we made in the liberation from imperialism is now surrendering to a curious variety of colonialism. There must be a massive movement for a Cabinet to rule India by a little man only because they are in search of a few votes in Parliament. We must have a better understanding of Parliamentary Government and majority rule. The Government of India to be ruled by a little local party is boloney. We require national stature, national policies and record of national Government and politics before handing over the country's rule to a person whose major policy is anti-BJP. I have nothing against Mulayam, his sin never in power before is the Chief Minister of U.P. replacing a lady who had a huge majority who lost because of the numerous statues structured herself. Little man and large Governments go ill together. India, *i.e.* Bharat has a great culture and must be ruled by one who has international reputation. Alas, from Jawaharlal Nehru and Indira Gandhi to Mulayam Singh and his son. What a fall! Merely to avoid general national election. Dr. Manmohan Singh has made India small. Oh, the pity of it!

Freedom Should Become A Colossal Colony

When the first Britisher in an imperial odyssey sailed from Britain to India with an imperial design landed in Kerala, occupied a small territory of India with the power of the British gun and the unwitting surrender of Bharat's sovereignty by the Zamorin of Calicut. India hardly knew that by gradual infiltration the native Princess over 600 of them would be victims of the British Crown and become a colony of the British Empire. However, from stage to stage 'We, the People of India' surrendered our freedom and became a colossal colony. The west conquered our glorious culture and the British masters made us their subjects. But the Indian people awoke and by a paradox of history a Britisher A.O. Hume started a political movement by forming the Indian National Congress. Great patriots like Dadabhai Naoroji, Balgangadhar Tilak and Sardar Vallabhai Patel built up a powerful national political party, the Indian National Congress. India was great although its culture had collapsed by the Congress political awakening a dynamic swaraj vision became awful and fought for our swaraj. We campaigned in Britain and in India for Poorna Swaraj and won. The British Parliament gave back Indian Freedom and Free India was born on the 15th August, 1947 by a historic declaration made by Jawaharlal Nehru. A Constituent Assembly was set up of Free India minds and thinkers and a socialist secular democracy with full sovereignty as a Republic came into being. The native Princess disappeared and the little Indians in billions secured political power. Swaraj in its grand dimension established its original culture. Max Muller, the German Philosopher wrote about the great Indian culture thus:

If we were to look over the whole world to find out the country most richly endowed with all the wealth, power, and beauty that nature can bestow – in some parts a very paradise on earth – I should point to India. If I were asked under what sky the human mind has most fully developed some of its choicest gifts, has most deeply pondered over the greatest problems of life, and has found solutions of some of them which well deserve the attention even of those who have studied Plato and Kant – I should point to India.

However, this cultural splendor and political freedom was expressed in the Preamble to the Constitution which wrote the vision of swaraj thus:

WE, THE PEOPLE OF INDIA, having solemnly resolved to constitute India into a SOVEREIGN SOCIALIST SECULAR DEMOCRATIC REPUBLIC and to secure to all its citizens:

JUSTICE, social, economic and political;

LIBERTY, of thought, expression, belief, faith and worship;

EQUALITY of status and of opportunity;

and to promote among them all

FRATERNITY assuring the dignity of the individual and the unity and integrity of the Nation.

This grand ideology was not fulfilled because our patriotic mission did not rise to the challenge of swaraj. Step by step the great glory of Indian swaraj which dominated our villages slowly sank into feudal slavery. Our economy failed, our swadeshi suffered the syndrome of foreign rule. British corporations occupied our economy everywhere. We lost our economic independence and everything was English speaking. The United States had become a world power after World War-I and India became a *de facto* American colony. Kerala itself was no longer independent but was an emerging colony of the English speaking world. Our village economy collapsed and even our towns and cities hardly remain Indian. Our national politics has a limitation of the British rule. Our villages have shed their Panchayati Raj and were merely feudal. Our Rashtrapati and Governors had no longer remained swadeshi but look to London for precedence. Our people became more impoverished. This syndrome of subordination finds resistance. But those who resisted were called Naxalites and Maoists to be suppressed by the Indian Army. Our national economy suffered and our swaraj no longer remained the great Indian kingdom. The socialist, secular declaration of the Constitution remained a paper promise and capitalism and colonialism became the ruling cult.

Indian politics rarely remains Indian and largely our governance under foreign influence. Our jurisprudence was borrowed from Anglo-American forces. Even our human rights are no longer original but adapted from ideas of Washington and London. Law India and Justice India and Economy India had an alien complexion. Indigent has aggravated. Expectations of swaraj darkened into anxiety, anxiety into dread, dread into despair and despair into terrorism. Our politics is no longer free. It is commercial and money is power and controls all public institutions. India and Swaraj are facing a crisis. We need a struggle to revive and survive who lives if India dies, who dies if India lives. This mission has to wake up with a passion. Do or die until our Constitution ideal of socialism, secularism and democracy are a reality. Our independence and our cultural originality have a global wonder to gain which should be a national battle. Beyond party politics and an egalitarian secularism becomes the rule of life and fundamental principles of administration.

The historic odyssey which narrates the story of the British conquest of India began in 1757. The first Indian arrested by the British in 1917 is Mahatma Gandhi and in exercise of British authority over India by 1947 India threw the British out and won its swaraj. The battle of Plassey was the first by the British who defeated Indian soldiery largely because Indians were disunited. From then on the British Empire took roots in India and we became a colony. The first National Anthem 'Vanthematharam' was composed by Bankim Chandra Chatterjee and sung by Rabindranath Tagore. Tricolour flag first flew in the skies and proved India a national power. The three colours are saffron, white and green. Saffron represents courage and sacrifice, White—Purity and Truth and Green—Faith and Fertility. We defeated the British not by arms but by non-violence, *Satyagraha* movement and the *Dandi* march (Salt Satyagraha) demonstrated. We won without weapons and by adopting the marvellous principles such as truth and non-violence and the glorious culture and values of India represented by Kohinoor. The world's finest honour is still with the British till that is returned and adorned the Indian capital our swaraj is not complete. Swadeshi economy is our national pride but does not even now in full splendor.

The greatest National Congress with its swaraj vision and political might resisted British power and made the Parliament grand. India its freedom and by Indian independent act liberated Bharat. A Constituent Assembly was set up and under Constitution made India a socialist, secular, democratic Republic. No more 'Lord Mountbatten" as the Viceroy who was replaced by the President of India with an Indian Parliament composed of members elected by the ballot of the Indian masses. Every Indian has a vote and democracy became a political reality. In Winston Churchill's words: the little man, walking into a little booth, with a little pencil, making a little cross on a little bit of paper – no amount of rhetoric or voluminous discussion can possibly diminish the overwhelming importance of the point."

Human Rights and the Common Citizen

How the universe came into existence is beyond me or anyone else to guess. But we find around us a Creation consisting of planets and other environmental factors. Among them by a process of evolution and in infinite period, has sprung the creature called man. Humanity in its collective form has to come to terms with environment. Otherwise we won't survive. Thus we find two factors, that every human being to survive has to be a citizen on earth which is the planet known to be the habitat of humanity. Any study of the survival of the human species must therefore has to focus on human rights *vis-à-vis* the common satisfaction. Citizenship involves the process of reconciliation of life with environment. Any discussion of this reconciliation process is possible only if we have a grasp of the ecology and submission of life to the ecological condition.

The world was born as plants first, then minerals, then agriculture and green environment. This green creation by imperceptible degrees developed into vegetables, insects, animals and birds and by magical creative processes blossomed into that colourful current cosmos. Man is the final product of this advance invested with that power called intellect. Thinking human beings moved all over the earth like the bud blossomed into flowers and gardens. Humanity developed from agriculture to higher forms of creative wonders reacting to that remarkable drive of divinity. Thus came into existence the universe which is the habitat of Life from insects to the molecular to molar forms of nature, we now call Creation. Man born in peace, happiness, vegetable culture, evolved technology, industry manifesting into the present civilization. The European Man developed the art of commercializing all arts and industries. It was the White Man who cultivated Material Power. The other continents like Asia by contrast turned spiritual and unfolded that inner being called the soul in its infinite depths. Thus we evolved the material and the spiritual dimensions of society. India excelled in the marvel of the spirit while London and Washington the white world transformed the earth into material universe. Science and Technology multiplied the industrial development while looking into the inner self and meditating like the Buddha and Gandhi, Asia developed philosophy and spirituality. There is now a profound subtle rivalry between the material dimensions of creation and the soul (meditation the thought process and the inner joy with the soul in its boundless fathoms). The world of material power belongs to the industrial culture while the trans mortal belongs to philosophers and thinkers who mostly survive in the East. The West is superior since the soul must finally submit to commercial might. This contest between the West and the East is the battle of the present world. The Third World has no gun or military power or material wealth. Barbarity versus morality of the celestial dimension of creation is what divides the world today. The Buddha, the Awakening One is in the East. The grand material glory with its crazy attraction over the five senses conquers the ascetic values.

The Fundamental development and difference between the barbarian culture of primitive Mankind and later cultural progress is the universal recognition by the modern civilization of the ideology of human rights the world over and the world legal order which will be realized through the World Justice Order which internationally finds acceptance in Peace and War. Each nation in finer fulfillment of this higher cosmic desideratum makes human rights as a paramount and integral part of the cosmic rule of law. Sans such a splendid rule of law that nation is barbarian. Humanity in its cultural odyssey towards its moral march and advance must have Rule of Law as impregnable and inalienable dimension of its Rule of Life absent which it is doomed to be in asuric depths. Most nations which belong to the international community have specific justice provisions in this behalf. They start from the dawn of culture from Greece, Rome the White Man's continent and Commonwealth earth. They are the Magna Carta of every advanced country. Even during War there are inviolable rules which are binding or else they are regarded as savage not human. It behoves the UNO to make the cosmic conscience, a code of human rights an integral part of Humane Jurisprudence. This is a Chapter of the World Charter of Justice. Even an imperial order like the British Empire is governed by its membership of the UN to abide by Human Rights. The UK, the USA and the Commonwealth countries and even colonies submit to

Human Rights. This is cosmic comity which binds every member of the United Nations and earlier a League of Nations as it came into Existence after World War-I and II. Today global Constitutions construct these rights as part of their Constitutions. Take, for instance the battle for American Independence and abolition of colonial status after the Boston Tea Party which initiated a Civil War waged by the Americans and they won their Freedom. So too India by its do or die struggle for Swaraj.

Human rights are commonly understood as "inalienable fundamental rights to which a person is inherently entitled simply because she or he is a human being." Human rights are thus conceived as universal (applicable everywhere) and egalitarian (the same for everyone). These rights may exist as natural rights or as legal rights, in both national and international law. The doctrine of human rights in international practice, within international law, global and regional institutions, in the policies of States and in the activities of non-governmental organizations, has been a cornerstone of public policy around the world. The idea of human rights States, "if the public discourse of peacetime global society can be said to have a common moral language, it is that of human rights." Despite this, the strong claims made by the doctrine of human rights continue to provoke considerable skepticism and debates about the content, nature and justifications of human rights to this day. Indeed, the question of what is meant by a "right" is itself controversial and the subject of continued philosophical debate.

In the aftermath of the Second World War the Universal Declaration of Human Rights was proclaimed in Paris by the United Nations General Assembly in 1948. Thus, human rights in its authoritative formulation sprang from European secularization of Judeo-Christian ethics. The modern sense of human rights can be traced to Renaissance Europe and the Protestant Reformation, alongside the disappearance of the feudal authoritarianism and religious conservativism that dominated the Middle Ages. The Twelve Articles (1525) are considered to be the first record of human rights in Europe. In the 19th century, human rights became a central concern over the issue of slavery.

> "We hold these truths to be self-evident, that all men are created equal, that they are endowed by their Creator with certain unalienable Rights, that among these are Life, Liberty

and the pursuit of Happiness." – United States Declaration of Independence, 1776.

In the history of human rights the British Barons asserted their human rights against the arbitrary rule by King John. Lord Denning described it as "the greatest constitutional document of all times – the foundation of the freedom of the individual against the arbitrary authority of the despot. Indeed, this fight against arbitrariness influenced Mahatma Gandhi in South Africa. When Mohandas K. Gandhi led a mass burning of Indian registration cards in South Africa in 1908, a British newspaper compared the event to the Boston Tea Party. When Gandhi met with the British viceroy in 1930 after the Indian salt protest campaign, Gandhi took some duty-free salt from his shawl and said, with a smile, that the salt was "to remind us of the famous Boston Tea Party". The Magna Carta was a great event in the history of human rights all over the world. After the Magna Carta, the great constitutional event which triggered the American Revolution against British imperialism and its power to tax by a body not representing the people to be taxed. This was the Boston Tea Party movement which led to the American Revolution the history of this battle against Briton is a mighty event which revolutionized American resistance to British claim to impose tax upon its colonies. Indeed, these events had global impact and occupy a high place in the development of human rights.

There are many other aspects of human rights which require exploration and incorporation in the body of human rights jurisprudence. For example, Victimology is the scientific study of victimization, including the relationships between victims and offenders, the interactions between victims and the criminal justice system — that is, the police and courts, and correction officials — and the connections between victims and other social groups and institutions, such as the media, businesses, and social movements. Victimology is however not restricted to the study of victims of crime alone but may include other forms of human rights violations. Abolition of any inequality like social and economic injustice are areas of which country after country is making an integral part of its rule of law. Human right is not a static idea. But advances into new value systems. Abolition of slavery, gross economic inequality and acceptance of socialism, democracy with universal adult franchise plus, plus are gaining adoption even in the Dark Continent. Criminal jurisprudence focused mostly on crimes and punishment for it. This is writ large in the Indian Penal Code. The victims of crimes do not get reparation by the mere punishment of the offender. Criminal justice to be fair and complete must compensate the victims by making the offender pay or otherwise other punishments alone will not give adequate satisfaction to the victim. This grave deficiency is made good by victimology where the penal law not merely punishes the offender but makes the victims receive a sense of solace by cash compensation or other forms of adequate justice. Gender egalite, abolition of colour bar which Chief Justice Earl Warren brought into USA by his great judgment and the abolition of death sentence in some countries has an impregnable defence of the right to life. The great Rio de Janeiro rights are some of the examples where human rights are expanding their jurisdiction.

There are two basic conceptions of environmental human rights in the current human rights system. The first is that the right to a healthy or adequate environment is itself a human right (as seen in both article 24 of the African Charter on Human and Peoples' Rights, and article 11 of the San Salvador Protocol to the American Convention on Human Rights). The second conception is the idea that environmental human rights can be derived from other human rights, usually – the right to life, the right to health, the right to private family life and the right to property (among many others). This second theory enjoys much more widespread use in human rights courts around the world, as those rights are contained in many human rights documents. Freedom of thought, freedom of speech, freedom of association, freedom from slavery and torture inside even prisons are some of the newer developments of human rights. Relativism and universalism which are still moot issues debated amongst scholars today. This shows that human rights are an expanding ideology and are marching ever onwards into a world where man matters and his dignity gains greater value. Children's rights and Women's rights and even the rights of the child still in the womb are being included in the expanding universe of human rights. Defence of individual nations against nuclear menace (*vide* Hiroshima, Nagasaki, Chernobyl and Three Mile Island) and other lethal scientific discoveries are now necessary as part of the right to life of people of backward nations.

Human rights are a condition of human dignity. No human rights make life worthwhile unless there is a purpose for which we live and the process by which we achieve that purpose. In short, the ends and means are both important. To achieve the ends of universal creation we require appropriate means and this link up between the ends and means is management. Sans management ends can never be reached. The means must be designed which will take the living being to the desired goal. This is management, sans management existence ends in chaos. Order is necessary if society is not to end up in chaos. So we must have in all universities scholarship studies and scientific pursuits as an integral part of the development of efficient management. The study of management is a subject integral to the totality of University studies. Unfortunately sufficient stress is not given to the quality of management and so efficiency of management is absent in administration and the world is facing the collapse of efficiency and the bankruptcy of handling any process of life. The rule of law can never succeed unless it is an excellent means to fulfill the objectives of social justice. Rule of law is linked up with the rule of life. Bernard Shaw has stated in wise cynicism that 'He who can does, he who cannot teach us'. The incompetent when in authority takes on the role of teaching and unfortunately the incompetence breeds and corruption creeps in. Although democracy cannot be given up if people matter, said Bernard Shaw:

> 'Democracy substitutes election by the incompetent many for appointment by the corrupt few'.

Therefore democracy has to be elevated to standards of efficiency through a process of intelligent designs of management. Thus the Executive and bureaucracy will never be efficient without management. Elections are indispensible if democracy is to survive. Elections as instruments become purposeful if only there is a management study of the Houses. What we see today in the Houses is howling not deciding because the members are not inspired by sense of management but only of grabbing power. Power without efficient objectives ceases to be serving a democratic rule of law. The Legislature becomes a paralysed instrument without rules regulating the governance of the House. It often happens that members are at cross purposes and without a sense of harmony. Efficient administration of the Houses ceases to be a reality when the Executive and the Legislature malfunction. The judiciary is supposed to settle disputes and see that the Constitution functions through correct interpretation and enforcement of the provisions of the Constitution. But when the judiciary is not properly trained and produced added confusion by the *Ipse Dixit* of the ignorant judges in their arrogance and arbitrary rule, the Judiciary and as such the democratic system as a whole also fails. Thus we find that the management of the Executive, of the Legislature, of the Judiciary are important if these three instruments of the State are to produce an orderly administration. In short, the paramount purpose of good democracy makes it obligatory to have management of each branch of administration with intellectual clarity and scientific methodology but *alas*, management itself requires refinement. Absent that, today if society is to enjoy good Governance, have the cosmos not to end up in chaos, high priority must be imparted to the study of management in the field of politics, public business and administration of the laws. The Executive becomes arbitrary, arrogant and authoritarian, absent the Legislature which is the people's voice to make the Executive democratic. The Legislature when geared to majority power ceases to be scientific, sensitive and didactic and can be fit only if there is an independent Judiciary truly learned and insightfully aware of the purpose of the Constitution. Thus, the Judiciary is all important in a democracy. The management of the Judiciary including the selection of judges and functioning methods is of key importance. Regrettably there is no law regulating the functionalism of the Judiciary itself. This failure leads to judicial conflicts, poor selection and sometimes ghastly performance and if the Judiciary fails, the Constitution collapses and the other two branches become menaces.

The present system in more parts of the Universe, the UK, the USA, the USSR with the Montesquean shape of trinity of instruments does not give the paramountcy or importance to Management and so the performance are a picture of caricature and negative performance, more sinned against than sinning. Management is business lacking in quality but Paramountcy is paramount. Well began is half done. The British King in Parliament has been the model for influencing the world of democracy whether of the USA, the USSR or the Commonwealth countries. But their Viceroy in Delhi was a picture of abuse of power perfunctorily controlled by the Commons. How ghastly the abuse was during Warren Hastings Viceroy was seen during the Impeachment of Hastings! Burke spoke:

> 'I impeach him in the name of the people of India, whose rights he has trodden under foot, and whose country he has turned into a desert. Lastly, in the name of human nature itself, in the name of both sexes, in the name of every age, in the name of every rank, I impeach the common enemy and oppressor of all!'

We have little Hastings in numbers in many States in India too. One of the Statesmen of the Indian Parliament Dr. Manmohan Singh is now charged and his resignation demanded by the BJP and exposed in the Washington Post. Every Panchayat has little Hastings. Pity! Because there is no Business Management, no Independent Judiciary, no Public Interest Litigation, nor article 32 at the District Court level. Indeed, there is but a few management institutions. . . . . *sine qua non* for every large public office. Business Management must be introduced in Public Service Commissions and audit-trained personnel in every large administrative office so that there is internal trained audit and business management in every public office from Panchayat to State and Central Administration. Time and tide wait for no man. So too the District auditor professionally trained, Business Management officials in every large Public Office with immunity and independence. There then will be an Operation Transformation.

A Case for Sad Serious Investigation for the Nation's Constitutional Preamble's Sake

A popular English daily published from Kochi on the 12th September, 2012 discloses exceedingly alarming news by a well-known commentator Mr. S. Gurumurthy.

What is well-known is that there is a sublime lady Matha Amrithanandamayi whose Ashram is near Kollam, lovely and near the backwaters. I had visited the Ashram only once, met Mathaji only once and found a peaceful lady. Very simple and her whole life seems committed to serve society through hospitalization and educational colleges and other allied institutions of repute. Of course, she has such institutions in Kerala which has essentially Hindu ethos but I have not seen a trace of communalism in the hospitals or the medical staff or the nurses who are a militant lot who had recently won a strike for dignity and descent emoluments. Condensing a five column article in a leading English daily which is disturbing to read but more than that raises issues against the Government and its police establishment. Certain disturbing questions raised in the article are matters of public importance. I wonder whether the Government is sensitive enough to investigate the points raised and whether any policy decisions have been reached to assure secularism, public peace and elimination of lunatic hostility by Islamic values. If it has, it should be given due publicity because more than Mathaji and the rising trend of infiltration of Islam into public institutions we must have the Preamble to the Constitution and its values like integrity, fraternity, liberty, equality, justice, social and economic as fundamental in the governance of the country. If the Government neglects its duty chaos, terrorism and corruption can abound and after a time their behavioural barbarities may become beyond Khaki control. This is not a matter of concern of Mathaji's institutions alone but breed fowl on the sentiments of Hindus and in turn, of communal rabid trends.

Dear Chief Minister, I regard you as a Statesman beyond narrow fanaticism and crass superstition.

Dear Prime Minister, I regard you too to be secular Statesman who came to Kerala and made a brief speech on Emerging Kerala. It is time that the Central and State Governments alert themselves on subversive movement not merely in a Naxal or Maoist violence but also subversive movement propagating communal sentiments. No temple, no mosque, no church while free to function can be allowed to be agencies of terrorism. A stitch in time saves nine. Now Dear Chief Minister and Prime Minister take up a national investigation at the State and the Central level and discover what is latent in these bedlam movements. Have a Commission if necessary. What is in time today may be too late tomorrow. Will the media of national stature and vernacular publicity heed my appeal to ensure the culture of secularism? Today diversity of theology has made solidarity, humanity and divinity values on their way out and lunatic theology becoming rabid pathology. Hasten, arise, awake and stop not till socialism, secularism and democracy become impregnable forces in our polity. Satnam is not alone and is not dead nor is Bismillah eclipsed. Both are dangerously waiting for a fresh opportunity to display barbarity.

The Noble Preamble: We have Promises to Keep

Over a semi-centennial span ago We, the People of India, made a tryst with destiny to redeem every human being in our Republic from Poverty, Slavery, Inequality, Deprivation of Developmental Opportunity and Denial of Access to Justice in its well-known triune dimensions. More than five decades after, let us turn back to our nation's performance in an objective spirit of social audit and creative critique. The Indian humanscape, when Freedom dawned in August 1947, was vibrant with socialist hope of egalite, liberty and pursuit of happiness. As the 20th century was about to set and a new millennium was being midwifed by passage of time, the onward Nehruvian locomotion of people's progress took a reverse Manmohanomic direction with some authoritative estimate declaring, a decade after the Globalisation experiment, India to be the poorest country in the world. People's rosy expectations at the hour of Independence, darkened into indifference, indifference into blood and tears, which in turn, dismayed into the doom of despair. Of course, this sad scenario afflicted only the vast masses. The movement was zigzag and princelings, feudal elements, bourgeois sections and a noveau riche class emerged with consumerist appetite, imitative of the West and pejorative allergy to native culture. The great majority were harrowingly under-privileged and demanded alleviation of penury and elimination of unemployment and other privations. The antimony between the Proprietariat and the Proletariat deepened and hunger for socio-economic change hotted up. Meanwhile, human rights and democratic values, in their holistic dimensions, gained political voice and the Constitution largely reflected, given semantic radicalism, the militant desiderata of the deprived, preponderant population. We started well with the grand Preamble and the glorious verbiage of article 38 of the Constitution, setting the nation's sights socialist and secular, egalitarian and economically advanced. The crimson aspirations and libertarian transformation of the social order found finer expression through the early Constitutional Amendments, the reports of the left-oriented Planning Commission, nationalisation of Key industries, the creation of a public sector which was meant to occupy the commanding heights of the national economy, and a great stress on agrarian reform.

Judged by political rhetoric and stentorian polemics, our legislatures sounded radical and our courts, though at times darkly conservative, also supported progressive values. The Nehru-era was a proud beginning, notwithstanding *de facto* single Party politics, corruption in public life, misuse of Constitutional powers under article 356 and defeat at the hands of China. Indo-Soviet friendship, States reorganisation, independence of the judiciary and the stature of Jawahar as utterly secular, genuinely socialistic, keen on land reforms and leading the world movement for liberation of colonies and developmental march of the Non-Aligned Movement; were notable events which inspired confidence in the people about the realisation of the Indian revolution. But feudalism dies hard, colonial mentality resists constitutional liquidation and bureaucracy, habitually paper-logged and hierarchically structured, rarely bows out. So, Bharat continued to live simultaneously in several centuries.

Nehru, the leader of the Freedom Struggle, was a militant humanist but Nehru, the Prime Minister, was a Hamlet. His charisma suffered somewhat from the bar of limitation since his performance did not slough off the old world ethos or soft state syndrome. In nation-building civilian administration as supreme, the democratic order as basic and making socialist ideas and abolition of poverty with a vision and plan Nehru made headway and thereby strengthened liberty, equality and other fundamental rights of the lower layers of humanity.(The creamy layer and communal strata survived.) Secularism and socialism became vogue words even in high official circles and foreign economic infiltration or invasion were checked to some extent. Human Rights flourish only in such a milieu as Nehru verbally emphasised. A revolution needs cadres with political conviction and infrastructure deeply committed and a leadership defiant of imperialist powers and their next of kin who cunningly and corruptly do back-seat driving. Equality, liberty and other great freedoms summon echelons at all levels, including the professions, technical experts and visionaries with principled, planning pragmatism. Mao Tse Tung's two observations, absent under Nehru and the 'Leftists', but actively operational in New China, need recapitulation.

> *A revolution does not march in a straight line. It wanders where it can, retreats before superior forces, advances wherever it has room, attacks whenever the enemy retreats or bluffs and, above all, is possessed of enormous patience.*
>
> *Revolution is not a dinner party, nor an essay, nor a painting, nor a piece of embroidery; it cannot be advanced softly, gradually, carefully, considerately, respectfully, politely, plainly and modesty.*

The fatal failure of our fine Preamble and Nehru's red rose perspective have several causes. Etiologically perceived, the system was run by cadres and leaders for whom the common people hardly mattered and the 'old order' was preserved by a political and official elite conditioned by British *Raj* ethos and *Maharaja* bossism. The judicial fraternity too were of Indo-Anglian vintage. Left nomenclature, largely fabricated for winning elections, left the populace cold since poverty alleviation, employment generation and people's participation were discovered by the have-nots to be abracadabra. Disenchantment with gubernatorial duplicity and judicial inaccessibility compounded by Anglo-philic erudition, created extremist militancy and terrorist estrangement Result: High sounding Liberty – Equality-Development – vocabulary on the one hand and pervasive privation, escalating unemployment and illiteracy unlimited on the other. Of course, periodic elections, reeking with corruption and counterfeit-ballots, was a simulacrum of democracy. True, Winston Churchill was right when he observed: 'At the bottom of tributes paid to democracy is the little man, in a little booth, with a little pencil making a little cross on a little bit of paper—no amount of rhetoric or voluminous discussion can diminish the overwhelming importance of the point'. The same anti-Indian Churchill opposed handing over Independence to Indian leaders whom he described as 'rogues, rascals and freebooters'. Both his powerful statements, in retrospect, after 50 years of booth-capturing game and dubious governance deserve serious debate *vis a vis* liberty, equality and other democratic values. The Preamble prised open the precious values of human dignity, access to social, political and economic justice as well as liberty and other fundamental rights. But while in the early decades measures were taken to build the basic structure necessary for social justice to be a reality, abuse of power and ubiquity of corrupt politics and judicial conservatism grew without let or hindrance. Executive authoritarianism and irresponsible parliamentarian arrogance slept together, with liberal diction about people's power and socialist pattern being the opium of the people.

How fragile is our working anarchy and oligarchy alias Indian democracy has been poignantly presented with lucid emphasis by Dr. Ambedkar in the Constituent Assembly. Our Constitution is a majestic instrument and if implemented in letter and spirit the present generation would be placed a happy Administration. But asked Ambedkar on 25th November 1949: 'What would happen to her (India's) independence?.........Will she lose it a second time?.......... What perturbs me greatly is the fact that not only India has once before lost her Independence but she lost it *by the infidelity and treachery of some of her own people*...... Will history repeat itself? We must be determined to defend our independence to the last drop of our blood.' Later, in the course of his address, he placed accent on social democracy beyond political democracy. He clarified that liberty cannot be divorced from equality and fraternity. Equality without liberty would kill individual initiative. Without fraternity, liberty and equality could not become a natural course of things. He admitted the complete absence in our society of genuine equality. The prophetic words he uttered are worth repeating more than half a century later because his fears are proving true now. "On the 26th January 1950 we are going to enter into a life of contradiction. In politics we will have equality and in social and economic life we will have inequality......... How long shall we continue to live this life of contradiction?........ We will do so only by putting our political democracy in peril. We must resolve this contradiction....... or else those who suffer from inequality will blow up the structure of political democracy......' Common brotherhood, as against dichotomy among the people with caste and class division, is a *denial of fraternity*. Sans fraternity, 'equality and liberty will be no deeper than coats of paint.' A grammar of anarchy may be the consequence, he warned. All these prophetic portents are happening under our nose and the struggle for a new social order can be successful only by realization of the perils pointed out by the great Indian Ambedkar.

The decadence of our democracy is mired by pathos and bathos because the victims are voiceless and Power is an illusion for them. Elite are the privileged and thus there is none to protest when India is being recolonised and its freedoms are formal under dependencia syndrome. We have formally under a Constitution but by the grace of world corporatecracy, with American hegemony. Gandhi Swadeshi is dead. Nehru socialism is under eclipse. The Constitution is comatose and the Courts are drowned in oceanic litigation. Dalits have none to lead and there is chaos in the cosmos. The court itself has changed its class character. EMS was punished for contempt when he pointed out the class character of the judiciary but today the judicial class has secured larger emoluments, more power over the other two branches that justice, especially social justice, is in precarious condition. The past projects itself into the present and the tryst with destiny made by Indian's cannot be betrayed. A recap of a few pregnant Nehru passages is pertinent here:

> *Freedom and power bring responsibility. That responsibility rests upon this Assembly, a sovereign body representing the sovereign people of India. Before the birth of freedom we have endured all the pains of labour and our hearts are heavy with the memory of this sorrow. Some those pains continue even now. Nevertheless the past is over and it is the future that beckons to us now.*
>
> *That future is not one of ease or resting but of incessant striving so that we might fulfil the pledges we have so often taken and the one we shall take today. The service of India means the service of the millions who suffer. It means the ending of poverty and ignorance and disease and inequality of opportunity. The ambition of the greatest man of our generation has been to wipe every tear from every eye. That may be beyond us but as long as there are tears and suffering, so long our work will not be over.*

What, has happened to India through the semi-centennial spell? A.K.Goalan was detained without trial. Is this personal liberty? And what did the Court do after marathon arguments? They, by majority vote, upheld this incarceration. The fate of liberty remains vulnerable. The Court has often approved deprivation of personal liberty even as late as TADA. I do feel that Freedom of the masses, political or economic, is not safe in the hands of the Republic. Proof? The disastrous Emergency validated by the Supreme Court and the despotic irrational imposition of President's Rule on nine States twice and the Court lending its wax and seal and signature, legitimising the jettisoning of provincial autonomy. Over hundred times the precious State, though limited, sovereignty was overthrown with no judicial assertion against this contra-constitutionality.

The creation of a socialist order is a tough task, a battle against unconscionable capitalism. A public sector and nationalisation, abolition of Princes' Privy Purses and planned development holding under restraint concentration of wealth to the detriment of the people and distributive justice promotive of basic needs of the dire poor—these are fundamental requisites to fulfill the goals of the Preamble. But the Court struck down Privy Purses Abolition, Bank Nationalisation, Kerala Agrarian Reform and other progressive legislations, even Constitutional Amendments to protect certain progressive statutes. Indeed, the Court was to be guardian of people's liberties and be the sentinel on the *qui vive.* But on several occasions the judiciary gave the impression of being the conscience - keeper of the capitalist class. However, times changed and access to justice, formerly a difficult and expensive process, became easier with Public Interest Litigation becoming a democratic judicial remedy. Corruption was fought, abuse of power was struck down and environmental protection assured by judicial oversight. Human rights received special concern from courts. Custodial trauma or death, molestation of women, bonded labour, child labour and other harassments inside lock-ups and prisons found the judges sensitive watch-dogs with punitive sternness. Indeed, the Judiciary played a great part in defending life and liberty and sentencing violators of Human Rights. This massive task was executed by the court with such firmness that abuse of power by the Executive was checked making the authoritarian governments tremble because the 'robed brethren' had jurisdiction to control and condemn misdeeds by even high functionaries. The presence of Human Rights Commissions at National and State levels, Women's Commissions and juvenile justice processes have strengthened the people's rights although full powers have not been confirmed. The struggle for a New Social Order made headway because many NGOs sprang to move the judiciary and NHRC with responsive writs issuing from the higher tribunals and recommendations from Commissions. Moreover, the Court began to use even U.N. instruments and the Directive Principles of State Policy as effective hermeneutic, humanitarian aids to read municipal laws humanely. Human Rights Jurisprudence was deepened and broadened and access to justice, what with PIL and judicial activism, was 'in widest commonalty spread'. Refugee law, anti-torture justice, gender justice, prison jurisprudence, children's rights, poverty jurisprudence and the like made the court the sanctuary of the weak and the asylum of the oppressed. Time was when, in Tennyson's lines, courts, unapproachable for the humble, were no longer hallowed but "where blind and naked Ignorance delivers brawling judgments, unashamed, on all things all day long". But those by-gone days are replaced and the new juristic time is : 'ring out the old, ring in the new'! Indeed, Tennyson versified, lovely fashion, (of Britain but now of India as well) :

A land of settled government,

A land of just and old renown,

Where Freedom slowly broadens down

From precedent to precedent.

Our Republic, with an ancient composite culture and modern socialist texture, suffered a value torture in the 90s of the 20th century. Socialism slumbered in the Constitution, secularism slowly lost its vigour and re-colonisation 'red in tooth and claw' pressured the Mughals in Delhi to abandon the marvellous values of humanism and compassion and substitute them with globalization, liberalisation, privatisation and marketisation. Gandhicidal, Nehrucidal, winds began to blow and a 'New Democracy', shaped by exotic forces and corporate compulsions, made Bharat an international mendicant and GATT victim. Indeed, a constitutional coup secretly, silently infiltrated intriguingly into our economic vitals. A bizarre change of heart and head with quislings in power made India Westoxicated. Today, dollar hunger of the rich dominates; and starvation and hunger of the poor has ceased to be a matter of grave concern. Patriotism, Swadeshi and self- reliance are on a long holiday. What once was anathema and allergy because it was imperialist is now darling as dollar adventurism, disguised as technological venture. The gap between the rich and the poor is widening. Glitteratti are glad and imports are in profusion. Agriculture is collapsing and rural indebtedness and suicides are escalating. 'Fair is foul and foul is fair.' In particular, contra-constitutional forces have stultified the Preamble.

> *Political chemeleons must quit if swaraj is to be stable. Without social justice, no social stability will last longer than the waves that break upon the Bench and are absorbed by the sands. Now we seek*

> *stability and secularity plus corruption free social order. Whose democracy? Whose stability? Whose social justice? We, the people of India must call the bluff and end the 'progress' baloney of the proprietariat. (Andhra University Law Journal P-5)*

The dynamic rule of law has to reassert itself charging forward with the Preamble as the goal. Currently an 'iron curtain' has descended on the land between the people in their miserable millions and the richer tycoons collaborating with MNCS and mafia corruption. 'Quit India' has a new dimension and progressive direction. Today, when the people must be educated about their grim future if we do not change course and become a self-reliant fraternity with social and economic democracy, we will fail in the long run. Even foreign lawyers will force themselves in! In my humble view, to delay the reassertion of the Constitution and its Preamble may lead to recolonisation. That shall not be. Law is for Life—of a billion Indian humans.

The Hidden Agenda of the New World Order is satirically yet truthfully expressed by Steinbeck in an oft quoted observation representing the current Indian lot of blood, toil tears and sweat. I quote Steinbeck so as to open the eyes of great jurists who live far away from hungry realities:

> *The fields were fruitful, and starving men moved on the roads. The granaries were full and the children of the poor grew up rachitic, and the pustules of pellagra swelled on their side. The great companies did not know that the line between hunger and anger is a thin line.(The Pocket Book of Quotations P-144)*

The Bench and the Bar, do awake and break the chains using Judge Power as the sword of We, the People of India.

The Constitution Revisited

When Alladi Kuppuswami writes with erudition and with a panoramic vision of the Constitution I behold a sort of genetic genius in the pages since Alladi Krishnaswami Aiyar, the author's father, was among the most eminent makers of our nation's paramount Founding Deed. His constellation of essays are luminous, without being voluminous, persuasive without being pedantic and versatile without being blinkered. Constitutional law is the prince among the many branches of jurisprudence and Justice Kuppuswamy, cradled in the Alladi culture, has demonstrated his excellence in the field thro' the VIII parts of the book. And what is important, he has touched on a variety of topics on which the people seek light as they affect the basics of law and life. In this single volume, Kuppuswami has omitted scarcely any currently relevant constitutional issue. And he touched none that he did not adom. His very approach is people-oriented.

> *The Preamble to the Constitution emphasises the fact that it is the work of the people of India and the Constitution loses all its meaning if it is not understood by the people. I hope this publication will serve the purpose of educating the people of India on some important constitutional questions.*

The book begins with a chapter on the framing of the Constitution. Reading the passages we re-live the Constituent Assembly proceedings. This has become possible because the author himself, son of that jurist statesman Alladi Krishnaswamy, was sitting in a corner of the lobby of the Constituent Assembly watching avidly the debates from start to finish. It must have been a great experience for a young man to be a witness to the great debates. Rightly the Author pays a great tribute to Dr. Ambedkar than whom none higher sat in the drafting committee and the open assembly. Remember that the others were giants and amidst them this *mahan Manu* shone as a mastermind shaping the destiny of India.

Many controversial questions have attracted Kuppuswami's attention. For instance, should we shift to the Presidential system? The author expresses himself without equivocation:

> *Views have been expressed by some jurists that parliamentary democracy has been a failure and must be replaced by the presidential form of government prevailing in the USA. If the parliamentary system has not functioned satisfactorily it is not due to any defect in the system but due to the incompetence or inefficiency of those who have been running the system. One of the obstacles to the success of federalism and parliamentary democracy in India is the proliferation of political parties, particularly on a regional basis. The existence of two major parties is the ideal for the working of parliamentary democracy. For a coalition to function successfully, the parties must combine for a particular purpose and sink their differences. They must be clear about the common objective and a common dominating purpose. Sri C. Rajagopalachari was also of the view that normally the existence of a two-party system in which each of the big political groups possesses effective and continuous leadership is conducive to the successful working of parliamentary democracy. Even in USA an eminent jurist has compared the Presidential form of government when the President belongs to one party and the majority of the Congress and the Senate to another party, to a motor car having two steering wheels operated by two drivers in which case no one knows in which direction the motor car will move. Dr. Ambedkar said in his speech that parliamentary democracy is not the only ideal form of democracy but it was the best under the circumstances. He, however, added that his anxiety about the future of India "was deepened by the realisation of the fact that in addition to our old enemies in the form of castes and creeds we are going to have many political parties with diverse and opposing political creeds.*

Dealing with many polemical problems the Author quotes Granville Austin:

"The members of the Assembly drafted the Constitution that expressed the aspirations of the nation. They skillfully selected and modified the provisions they borrowed, helped by the experts among their number... The Assembly members also applied to their task with great effectiveness two wholly Indian concepts, consensus and accommodation. Accommodation was applied to the principles to be embodies in the Constitution. Consensus was the aim of the decision-making process, the single, most important source of the Constituent Assembly effectiveness." May these two principles of accommodation and consensus guide our leaders in these difficult and troublous times.

Towards the end of his speech, presenting the Draft Constitution, Dr. Ambedkar rightly pointed out that we must not be content with political democracy; we must have social democracy also, which recognizes liberty equality and fraternity as the principles of life. On the economic plane there are some who have immense wealth as against men who live in abject poverty. He lamented, "How can people, divided into several thousands of castes, be a nation? The sooner we realize we are not as yet a nation in the social and psychological sense of the word the better for us."

I have maintained as my emphatic axiom that the Preamble to the Constitution has a pre-eminent place in the understanding and interpretation of the articles of the Constitution. Indeed, it is an integral part of the Constitution, whatever the pedantic lucubration of scholars might assert to the contrary. Justice Kuppuswamy has examined the Preamble and its implications for national integration. "We, the people of India," – a grand idea – is the comucopia of the constitutional ideology. The author has spelt out from the Preamble the plural implications and fall-out of human rights. He appeals with justification:

Every young person should be asked to commit to memory the Preamble to the Constitution and strive to preserve the unity and integrity of our country. The elders should set an example for the youngsters to follow by sinking all their differences based on caste, community, region and religion. In particular the politicians and administrators should not exploit communal, caste or regional differences for their selfish ends and should endeavour to bring about national integration.

Is Indian a Federation or a quasi-federation or a mere unitary State? Here comes the Centre and State relations, the claim to autonomy by different communities of the Northeast, the demand for Uttarkhand *etc.* The Author quotes Prof. Wheare to say that:

> *It is not enough if you have the right type of federal Constitution, you must have also the capacity and the will to work it satisfactorily. If not you will have a federal Constitution but will not have a federal govt. That capacity and the will is unfortunately lacking in the politicians of today. It is hoped that there will be a change in their attitude and wise counsel will prevail and we will in a short time achieve the equilibrium between national integration and state autonomy.*

There is a comparative study of the Constitution of India and the USA. Every student of constitutional law must read this chapter because the learned author has brought out the essential features of the two constitutions, a grasp of which is necessary if the Indian jurist is to speak with authority on federal issues. These are now being fought out by the people in the country. In this context the chapter on federalism in India and Canada is also instructive. It is surprising that a traditional lawyer, elevated to the Bench, dealing with the municipal laws and certain articles of the Constitution has been able to spread the wings of his juristic interest wide to cover what is usually left to academe.

Right from the beginning the Supreme Court has considered the importance of fundamental rights and the status of directive principles of state policy. Justice Kuppuswamy has, under various chapters dealt with this broad subject in part IV of his volume. Secularism has fallen for his consideration and he concludes a chapter dealing with the subject thus:

> *I can do no better than end this article with a quotation from the speech of Sri M. Ananta Sayanam Iyernga (who was the speaker of the Lok Sabha) during the debates in the Constituent Assembly: "I look forward to that day when humanity will be one, when all castes and creeds will disappear, (Cheers): When children are asked as to what religion they belonged, they may say, 'I do not belong to any religion but I am an Indian and do take pride in being one'. I would amend this last sentence as follows—The children may say "It does not matter which religion I belong—I am an Indian and I am proud to be an Indian."*

It is not my purpose to prolong this foreword since my task is only to introduce the book through a prolegomenon. The meaty matter is extensively covered in the book.

Members of parliament sometimes fail to be present in the House with the result that even the quorum is not available. Dereliction, but can't help. What happens to legislation passed by a House without a quorum? Kuppuswamy gives the answer.

> *Even if the validity is not liable to challenge it is not in consonance with democratic traditions to have on the Statute book an Act passed in the absence of a quorum. The quorum is prescribed at a meagre 10 per cent of the members. An Act passed at a meeting where the quorum is absent would be one passed on the basis of the votes of an insignificant number of members. Yet it will have the imprimatur of the whole House representing the entire body of the electorate. That is why as stated in May's Parliamentary Practice, quoted in the decision of the Federal Court referred to earlier in similar circumstances, Parliament in England proceeded to re-enact or validate the provisions of the doubtful enactment. The Indian Parliament would do well to adopt this procedure, imitating with advantage (in the words of Spens, J. in the case referred to earlier) the British Parliament. (The Hindu, Tuesday, February 17, 1987)*

The electoral reforms are being debated everywhere today while the polling processes are undergoing stress and strain and violence leaves the ballot process bloodstained. The learned author has his observations to make although I may not wholly agree with his conclusions. The question of President and Cabinet system deserves a second look, watching the distressing situation today. There are interesting ancedotes, which enliven the book such as we find in the chapter headed the Bhandari story. On the whole, I deeply appreciate Justice Kuppuswamy on the Constitution and regard it as a valuable contribution to Indian Constitutional Literature.

The Judicial Process and Delivery of Social Justice

If a free society cannot help the many who are poor, it cannot save the few who are rich' (Clement Atlee). In India, the Constitution specifically argues for egalite and against concentration of wealth which operates to the detriment of the public.

I am aware that the omnipresence, omniscience, and omnipotence of Money Power makes our pluralist society's Project Social Justice and strategy of Planned Development more a matter of political stratagem than credible realism. The disease of corruption, in its widest connotation, has affected all parties, and even militant organisations, although substantial differences in degree and opportunity may exist. The purity and neutrality of the Judiciary itself is in jeopardy. Again, even the militants who sloganise 'workers of the world, unite', oblige the enemy by practising the motto: 'workers of India, disunite'. Kilkenny cat radicalism has ruined Indian socialist prospects and even Naxalites self-divide, defeat and temporize with vices like communalism and regionalism for the sale of 'power'. Constitutional power is guided by/Constitutional values. The core creed of the Constitution and the nation's need has been spelt put by Nehru long ago:

> *Our final aim can only be a classless society with equal economic justice and opportunity to all, a society organized on a planned basis for the raising of mankind to a higher material and culture level. Everything that comes in the way will have to be removed, gently if possible, forcibly if necessary. And there seems to be little doubt that coercion will often be necessary.*

Social Justice through Public Interest Litigation and judicial activism is the phenomenal success story of our time although PIL abuses are creeping into this methodology and judges use PIL power against the poor!

> *I repeat....that all power is a trust—that we are accountable for its exercise—that, from the people, and for the people, all springs, and all must exist.' This Disraeli truism is the fundamental faith of every authentic Republic.*

The Indian Constitution turned to this democratic commitment begins its Preamble thus:

> *WE, THE PEOPLE OF INDIA, having solemnly resolved to constitute India into a (SOVEREIGN SOCIALIST SECULAR DEMOCRATIC REPUBLIC) and to secure to all its citizens:*
>
> *JUSTICE, social economic and political;*
>
> *LIBERTY of thought, expression, belief,*
>
> *EQUALITY of status and of opportunity;*
>
> *and to promote among them all*
>
> *FRATERNITY assuring the dignity of the individual and*
>
> *The (unity and integrity of the Nation);*
>
> *IN OUR CONSTITUENT ASSEMBLY this twenty sixth day of*
>
> *November, 1949, do HEREBY ADOPT, ENACT AND GIVE TO OURSELVES THIS CONSTITUTION.*

There are three great instrumentalities which have to make this profound promise an authentic reality. The Legislature makes laws, the Executive implements them or issues commandments until laws replace them and the Judicature interprets and adjudicates so that the Constitution-in-action may fulfil the dreams and aspirations of the Founding Fathers who sought to express in powerful words, the paramount purposes of the vast masses of Bharat. Apparently the least dangerous but actually the most authority-vested of the three constitutional agencies is the judicature. Finality is given to the rulings of the Supreme Court which are binding on all courts and civil authorities which are bound to aid the decisions pronounced by judicial adjudication. Sans the purse and the sword, the court still is the highest in which the Founding Fathers have invested the largest reservoir of power. While the Cabinet is controlled by the Parliament, which in turn is answerable to the people at the polls, the court is independent, as it should be, uninfluenced by extraneous forces or internal pressures. The judges, high and low, transform the social order and give justice—social, economic, political and cultural, in such manner that the people secure what was promised to them by the noble Preamble. The confidence in the court system depends largely on the Judiciary in this sense, judges in their personal life as well as while on the Bench, must, like Caesar's wife, be above board. The dress and forms of address of Their Lordships are obsolete and the servile language used in court while making 'submissions' go to the head of those on the Bench arcanely suggesting that the law is a mystique, too esoteric for the laity to grasp. All professions, in a sense, are a conspiracy against laity (Bernard Shaw). Judges, like others, are instruments under the Republic of India, not under the Crown as of old. Judge Jerome Frank was critical of court attire, which he called the cult of the robe.

> *Wigs and gowns and other types of legal ceremony, encourage legal pomposity and distance courts from common standards and common sense. They imply to outsiders (and to insiders) that judges are not ordinary human beings whose conduct and statements are subject to normal standards of assessment and criticism. The protective clothing of the judge deters all but the most persistent critic. As one of Dicken's characters put it: 'Would you are a ha'penny for the Lord Chancellor if you know'd him in private and without his wig?—certainly not'.*
>
> (Judges pp.143-144).

Any custodian of power derived under the Constitution is necessarily accountable. Jerome Frank had insisted, like other great jurists, that every democratic institution (the Judiciary is one) must be transparent and accountable. Operators in the dark and engineers of power in secrecy are apt to be suspect like politicians. A judge, as Winston Churchill pointed out once in the House of Commons, is 'required to conform to standards of life and conduct far more severe and restricted than that of ordinary people'. Judges have to be independent so that their impartiality may be impressive. Indeed, the United Nations, in one of its instruments, emphasised the importance of judicial independence and laid down basic principles in that behalf. The demand for independence is not merely freedom from pressure of the Executive or other sources, but also from the personal prejudices, ancestral obsessions, aristocratic biases and class considerations. Personal predilections sometime warp the objectivity of judges who, like other humans, are necessarily subject to social limitations. Justice Cardozo, in his classic book on the Judicial Process, has stated that the great tides and currents which engulf the rest of men do not turn aside in their course and pass the judges by. A fair trial needs an impartial judge which is not always available on account of the social slants and other habits and interests, which have been dealt with in great details by Prof. Griffith in his well known book; The politics of the Judiciary:

> *The partiality that inevitably affects judges has been noted in cases with a political flavour. In 1911 Winston Churchill (then Home Secretary) told the House of Commons that 'where class issues are involved... it is impossible to pretend that the courts command the same degree of general confidence (as in other cases). On the contrary, they do not, and a very large number of our population have been led to the opinion that they are, unconsciously no doubt, biased. In 1920 Lord Justice Scrution made a similar point. He noted that judicial impartiality is difficult to attain. He was 'not speaking of conscious impartiality; but the habits you are trained in, the people with whom you mix, lead to your having a certain class of ideas of such a nature that, when you have to deal with other ideas, you do not give as sound and accurate judgments as you would wish'.*

The powers enjoyed by judges are co-terminus with their impartiality and independence. The appointments of judges must therefore be carefully done. Till recently, the highest Executive had the power to select judges to the higher courts. Now, it is taken over, in my opinion wrongly, by the top Judiciary. The judicial remuneration is high and prestige of justices great and immunity impregnable and consequential of some arrogance, undemocratic. In the USA, the Senate has a voice, sometimes exercised in an unruly fashion, although the selection is made by the President of the U.S. with the political eye. In England, the Lord Chancellor and the Prime Minister make the final selection often times mixing politics and expediency with other factors. In India, there is an iron curtain between the people on the one hand and the Bar and the Bench and the selection process on the other. The criteria for selection from the Bar to the High Court or Supreme Court are not clear. It is a dark room operation. Men with rich practice will not be guilty of social justice or empathy for indigence and must therefore be ruled out men or women with Anglo-American scholarship and allergy to

Indian legal thought, brainwashed by British Indian ideas, may not bother about the 'butcher, the baker and the candle stick maker' (Vivian Dose's vivid phrase) or the bonded labour, tortured gender or fettered prisoner. But when the affluent or princely glitteratti are taxed judges bend their will to wipe every tear from every such eye. Why? Because the judges today regard opulence as opium. When we total up all their salaries and perks plus Dives, not Lazarus move their heart. All these matters put them in a class above the commoners whose hunger for right and justice find them indifferent There are many exceptions whose compassion is moved by the working class and the marginalised humanity. So it is imperative that we define the criteria for selection of the judicial members with reference to Constitutional values. Those considerations must be integral to what the Constitution intensely indicates. The class and antecedents and political philosophy and social vision must be sternly identified.

However these considerations and the institutional values they reflect receive little attention in practice with the result that judicial appointments continue to dominate forensic discourses. It is necessary in the interest of constitutional clarity to identify the criteria and the norms and procedures that should govern appointments to judicial posts. The performance of judges must be open to criticism constructively not viciously, creatively, not to debunk the process of justice. Corruption cannot be left unexposed merely because such exposure may affect the institution. It is the other way about.

The Indian Judiciary is not openly political, unlike the American, who vote often politically as in the recent Al Gore-Bush Presidential litigation. The credibility of the Court is a great value. The access to justice, the faith in fundamental rights and social justice and the maintenance of the rule of law turn on judicial integrity, secularity, competency, socialist mentality and freedom from class, communal, sex and other plural inclinations. At a time as now, when the MNCs and their Corporate Quislings are operating an economic coupe against the sovereignty and human rights compassion of the Constitution, the Court is the guardian of secularism and socialism and informational democracy. To jettison these norms in appointments, as now, is disappointment indeed. Judicial ethos must be on comradely terms with the humanism of the Constitution by which the 'robed brethren' take their oath of office.

Access to justice, basic to the implementation of every human right, makes the judicial role pivotal to constitutional functionalism. Now that Public Interest Litigation has broad-based, democratised and people-oriented *vis-a-vis locus standi* and affirmative action, the judges have to be vigilant, well informed about international treaties and double-speak globalisation and privatisation processes and pretences which are incompatible with the human rights and social justice norms of our Constitution must be flushed out by creative writs of court. The court is the sanctuary of Indian humanity in such a crisis and corruption sweeping over the country Judicial ethics, National Judicial Commission, liquidation of arrears of dockets, other delays and delinquencies of the judicature and subordinate staff, avoidance of silencing of criticism of infirmities of the Bench through exaggerated use of contempt power, discouraging of hankering after publicity and successful use of technology for facilitation of the court process and the exposure of the aberrations of the Bar are essential to preserve the integrity of judicial process rest public confidence in the efficacy and openness of the adjudicating process should be gravely undermined. These and other flaws and frauds, now escalating, must be and can be, arrested. Ethics of judicial conduct is urgently needed. A non-statutory beginning has been begun by former Chief Justice but it is far from satisfactory when we compare Judicial Codes in the US. and elsewhere.

> *Some politicians, and a few jurists, urge that it is unwise or even dangerous to tell the truth about the Judiciary. Judge Jerome Frank of the US Court of Appeals sensibly explained that he had little patience with, or respect for, that suggestion. I am unable to conceive… that, in a democracy, it can ever be unwise to acquaint the public with the truth about the workings of any branch of government. It is wholly undemocratic to treat the public as children who are unable to accept the inescapable shortcomings of man-made institutions.. The best way to bring about the elimination of those shortcomings of our judicial system which are capable of being eliminated is to have all our citizens informed as to how that system now functions. It is a mistake, therefore, to try to establish and maintain, through ignorance, public esteem for our courts.*
>
> *English judges have every reason to be proud of the quality of their performance and no reason to fear more extensive public knowledge and assessment of their work. Nevertheless, there are aspects of*

judicial administration—appointment, training, discipline, criticism, mysticism, and publicity—which hinder, or detract from, their ability to serve society. We need judges who are not appointed by the unassisted efforts of the Lord Chancellor and solely from the ranks of middle-aged barristers. We need judges who are trained for the job, whose conduct can be freely criticized and is subject to investigation by a Judicial Performance Commission; judges who abandon wigs, gowns, and unnecessary linguistic legalisms; judges who welcome rather than shun publicity for their activities.

(Judges-David Pannick)

Indian Judges too are respected and hold high standards. To command people's confidence is the need of the hour. The petty done, and the Undone Vast is the ground reality. Judicial vanity cannot cover up culpable failures; forensic creativity is the call of our times. Trading our Freedom for dollars and yens is a yen which must be nipped in the bud. Otherwise social justice will be vapid. Radical reform of the judicial process is the first national priority and justifies financial resources and other dimensions of judicial autonomy being given high consideration, so too research and development. Let us demystify the courts, tribunals and the judges and begin to 'tell the truth of their lies'. (Prof. Baxi adapting Pablo Picasso's words). This is the beginning of Project Processual Justice to the People. No Society can survive without a fair justice system. The protagonist of the Court Process is the Judge on the Bench. So the central figure—the judge—must be the focus of forensic reform. First things first if human rights are high on the nation's agenda.

The judicial paradigm is best expressed by Frankfurter:

A judge should be compounded of the faculties that are demanded of the historian and the philosopher and the prophet. The last demand upon him to make some forecast of the consequences of his action is perhaps the heaviest. To pierce the curtain of the future, to give shape and visage to mysteries still in the womb of time, is the gift of the imagination. It requires poetic sensibilities with which judges are rarely endowed and which their education does not normally develop. These judges must have something of the creative artist in them; they must have antennae registering feeling and judgment beyond logical, let alone quantitative, proof.

Our Constitution, its Preamble is the lodestar of Justice. As Earl Warren felicitously expressed:

> *Our judges are not monks or scientists, but participants in the living stream of our national life, steeing the law between the dangers of rigidity on the one hand and of formlessness on the other. Our system faces no theoretical dilemma but a single continuous problems: how to apply to ever-changing conditions the never-changing principles of freedom.*

The Indian judge must rise to the burning justice needs of our age. They can, given the training and technological and business management course plus discipline and ethics excel the best in any other country.

Judicial activism is no more a serendipity. It is the conscious fulfilment of the obligation implied in the oath of office of a judge. That is his discipline, his ethic; his tryst with the people of India.

Contempt Power—Utility or Futility

In recent times the population of contempt cases has been exponential and exaggerated so much that contempt proceedings glut the dockets of higher courts. There is something pathological in this phenomenal escalation. Either the judges are becoming hypersensitive in robed vanity venality and venom or the populace is losing die grace, reverence and credence they owe to that functionally finest institution in the Republic, the Judiciary.

Forgive my odd beginning of the review of a book on the Law of Contempt. *Sathyameva Jayate* (May Truth be victorious) is the sublime national motto and every political policy or judicial philosophy to the contrary is *bete noire*. Why? Because all law and justice must submit to the hermeneutic harmony of Truth and Justice as Bharat's lodestar. If truth be no defense to contempt charge because the 'robed brother' is the dubious delinquent, corrupt judges can escape from exposition of misconduct. Usually, the jural obscurantism that the plea of truth can be repelled from investigation by the theory fabricated by judges in their own self-interest that proof of violation of probity, guilty for the rest of the world, is impermissible in contempt cases is controversial, of the Judiciary which is the first to be free from misbehaviour. Is Independence of judicial office consistent with bribery, sex abuse, pernicious influences, and vices intolerable in a President and Prime Minister? The law is an ass if that be the jejune contempt jurisprudence.

Many authors fear to tread the 'truth' path of Contempt Law but Samaraditya Pal has faced the issue and, with a slant against the traditional view that truth of imputations is no defense, has cited extensively from the earliest ruling of the Supreme Court in

Ramkrishna Reddy's case and the redoubtable jurist Seervai's eloquent Constitutional Law. The latter has observed:

> *This raises the question whether truth is a defence to an alleged contempt of Court if a person, or the Press allege and publish proofs of the misbehaviour of a judge. The judgments of the Supreme Court are not in a tidy state. But a careful analysis of our Supreme Court judgments, and judgments of English and Australian Courts, shows that truth is, and*

must be a complete defence to allegations of bribery, corruption, bias and other misbehaviour of a Judge. To hold otherwise would be to nullify the provisions of articles 124(4) and (5) in a practical sense, for few people would expose themselves to being committed for contempt in order to bring a corrupt judge to book. *Secondly*, so to hold is to put the judges above the Constitution which expressly provides for the removal of a judge for proved misbehaviour.

However, truth is a casualty as a defense against Contempt Charge, which is a pity. The law is, *alas*! what the judges say it is. The large number of honest judges would wish the black sheep to be exposed. One judge of the Bombay High Court, finding a lady in court who had sought to influence him over the telephone and told him that the other judge on the Division Bench had already agreed to her suggestion, protested, got up from the Bench and histrionically sat *dharna* against the Bench hearing the case. The alleged sinner who was the senior Bencher, very capable and courageous otherwise, perhaps with a little weakness, resigned later. Judicial deviances can be controlled, not by banning Truth but by providing for *in camera* investigation by a high level body.

While I am gravely mindful of the potential for blackmail of judges by unscrupulous and corrupt litigants and blackguardly busybodies professionally flourishing on intimidatory use of mudslinging this, by itself, cannot be just, fair and sufficient as reasonable restraint to *black out all serious charges* as scurrilous. Truth about the court is in public interest. Let me quote David Pannick and Judge Jerome Frank in support:

> *Some politicians, and a few jurists, urge that it is unwise or even dangerous to tell the truth about the Judiciary. Judge Jerome Frank of the US Court of Appeals sensibly explained that he had little patience with, or respect for, that suggestion. I am unable to conceive... that, in a democracy, it can ever be unwise to acquaint the*

public with the truth about the workings of any branch of government. It is wholly undemocratic to treat the public as children who are unable to accept the inescapable shortcomings of man-made institutions... The best way to bring about the elimination of those shortcomings of our judicial system which are capable of being eliminated is to have all our citizens informed as to how that system now functions. It is a mistake, therefore, to try to establish and maintain, through ignorance, public esteem for our courts.

'English judges have every reason to be proud of the quality of their performance and no reason to fear more extensive public knowledge and assessment of their work. Nevertheless, there are aspects of judicial administration—appointment, training, discipline, criticism, mysticism, and publicity—which hinder, or detract from, their ability to serve society. We need judges who are not appointed by the unassisted efforts of the Lord Chancellor and solely from the ranks of middle-aged barristers. We need judges who are trained fort the job, whose conduct can be freely criticized and is subject to investigation by a Judicial Performance Commission; judges who abandon wigs, gowns, and unnecessary linguistic legalisms; judges who welcome rather than shun publicity for their activities.

What is a judicious blend is to subject *prima facie* unbecoming misbehaviour to a confidential process of top-level inquiry. Since the highest is not above the law and the lowest not beneath the law, a judicial deviancy Commission may be a happy half-way methodology. To suppress altogether is wrong. To say 'open sesame' to all vicious lies is horrendous. Yet read the great Frankfurter as convincing argument:

To say that the framers of the Constitution sanctified veiled violence through coercive speech directed against those charged with adjudication is not merely to make violence an ingredient of justice; it mocks the very ideal of justice by respecting its forms while stultifying its uncontaminated exercise.

The pathological exaggeration of imputations on the Judiciary shall never go unpunished. Nor shall delinquent judges, under a contempt cover-up gain immunity and escape transparency and accountability. The glory of the Judiciary is our national necessity.

Samaraditya Pal's Third Edition is an excellent work and is all the more useful since an expanded treatment is included relating to contempt of tribunals and Legislatures. The menace to free speech, a fundamental right, springs from the exaggerated, inventive and invasively vain legislators making hell inside the House and taking action against others on fancied charges. The prosecutor and judge are the same. The shame of it is our legislators' *de facto* colonial dependence on the House of Commons' privileges of long ago, 54 years after Independence. Our Parliamentarians are diligent in lucrative escalation of emoluments and deafening stridency in the well of the House, avoiding reasoned debate. If this competitive loudness is not contempt of the House, iris contempt of the Constitution, oath-bound though the members are.

The book under review is exhaustive and excellent and does justice to the title and to the Law Research Institute which has sponsored this work. The statutory law, the constitutional provisions and the case-law in profusion need a well-marshalled presentation, which is concise, clear and has a biblio-lovely get-up.

On a former occasion I have had the opportunity to go through this erudite work. Now I have glanced over again through the pages and I am more impressed that the author has dealt with the delicate, difficult subject with luculent, lucubrious success. The Contempt of Courts Act, 1971 is dealt with fairly well even as the Constitutional bearing on Contempt of Court and Legislatures has received just consideration. The titles deal extensively with the sub-topics, including the power of the Supreme Court and High Court to make rules. The appendixes give us rules framed by. Similarly, the Sanyal Commission report (necessary portion) has been given in the appendix. The discussion, as we go through the pages, refers also to the Commonwealth rulings and the Phillimore Committee Report. A brief quote from the Report is relevant:

> *The Phillimore Committee had recommended that truth should not be an absolute defence because the very presentation of such a defence might provide a platform for the repetition of the original assertions or allegations; it might provide a cover under which to rake up some damaging episode in a judge's past life. But the Committee was of the view that if an addition to proving the truth of the allegations the contemner could also show that the publication was for the public benefit, he should be entitled to an acquittal.*

The American Supreme Court has taken a far more liberal view because of its high priority for 'free speech' under the American Constitution. There is no doubt that the Commission for Review of the Constitution, now engaged in enlargement of fundamental rights and other provisions, will give serious consideration to contempt power because it impinges on articles 14, 19 and 21 plus. My view while on the Bench has been conditioned by a happy reconciliation between two values. The reverence that one owes to the dignity of the judicature and the latitude one shows to the dialectic of free expression.

My Supreme Court Days—A Wan Span or Years of Elan?

Called to the Bar way back in 1938, I sprang it to lawyerly life with great elan and lucrative practice as a junior in the chambers of my father V.V. Rama Aiyar, a leading member of the Tellicherry Bar. Young in age, but with propitious opportunities to cross swords with vintage wonders of the Malabar Bar and beyond, it fell to me to spend my vernal years in versatile professional life. Busy from the beginning, both at the Bar and in public life, I had a head start. A brief spell in distressing preventive detention, lonely behind bars, steeled my soul and broadened my bosom, A few years later, the smile of fortune changed the course of my life. I became an ML A in the Madras Assembly and on the Reorganisation of States, I was elected to the Kerala Legislature and was sworn in as Minister. A little over a couple of years as Minister in Kerala, with several challenging and creative portfolios and exciting political battles, made my administrative career a hectic chapter of colourful work and innovative excellence in several dimensions, with the public and the Opposition cooperating in giving shape to novel constructive projects with which I experimented. My intrepid mind and spotless conscience were a humane asset and education in experiential compassion. I humanised prisons and prisoners and used habitative strategies. The common people loomed large in my vision of Minister's obligations. With the Ministry's exit, I was back at the High Court Bar. Still I battled as an Independent candidate, supported by Left Parties, in State General Elections and cultivated winsome ways to woo voters. When defeated, I parted company with poll politics. Back at the Bar, the art of 'submissions' and diction of courteous assertions before opinionated and erudite justices were fruitful gains. Later, when 'elevated', to the Bench in 1968 (Kerala High Court), I sat with the same 'robed brethren', but a sharply different social philosophy marked me out as an unorthodox socialistic, people-oriented jurisprudent, unbound by obsolete precedents and fossil forensic praxis, innovating pragmatic processes and sensitising legal justice with substantive values. The Constitution, to me, ceased to be an idle Preamble and printed prolixity, but became a lodestar imparting living light to litigative law. I tried out odd experiments, which solaced my spirit and gave relief to victims. This was my approach while I was Minister for Law, Justice, Prisons and Social Welfare, and my social philosophy illumined my judicial tenure. My next spell was in Delhi.

A short term in the Gajendragadkar Law Commission was a good preparation before my ascent to the Supreme Court in July, 1973. My farewell to Judicial career and jurisdictional power was in November, 1980. From then on, without respite, I have treated my life as a functional public trust to be executed by social service and espousal of common causes, including giving legal aid and getting justice to the people who needed my assistance. My days, since leaving office, have been busier (free offer) than ever before and embracing public issues spread over the whole spectrum of Life, ignoring age. I am a human being and nothing that affects or afflicts anyone's life is alien to me. That is my humble creed and testament of Truth—a tryst with Destiny and Universal Divinity I seek to redeem.

What were the memorable events of my life as judge? What were my guiding goals I tried to practise on and off the Bench?

The *first lesson,* fundamental to life and law, that I learnt on the Bench, as I sat with Chief Justice Ray whose fraternal feeling and uninhibited brotherhood filled me with unusual freedom and self-confidence, *was humility without hubris and humanist hearing without 'high Bench' hauteur.* The *second value,* which touched my judicial heart, was the compassionate treasury of the Preamble to the Constitution, particularly its five opening words—We, the People of India—as the democratic imperative which bound me. *Thirdly,* do hear either side fairly, since courage and independence obligated me 'to give (even) the devil his due', whether he be in the right or in the wrong'. Again, a single judge's singular opinion may be opinionated verdict prone to be erroneous. So I realised that 'the joint judgment of three is worth much more than three times the judgment of one, unless he is a genius' (Learned Hand). Dissent, I thought, was speech to the future and duty to the present since 'judicial responsibility includes the task of exposing bad precedents. Judges are, or should be, their brother's keepers'. Among the last things I learnt was that 'perfect justice is a mirage. In the pursuit of the illusion of perfect justice, we jeopardize the justice that is within our grasp'. *Finally*, what I was taught at college as Cromwell's message holds good for a judge: Think it possible in the bowels of Christ that you might be mistaken'.

While on the Bench, I continued my public activities of lectures in support of people's causes and professional enlightenment with no conformity to conventions but with great care not to prejudice the finer freedom and sacred neutrality of my high office as judge. On the contrary, I, gained a larger constituency to serve. I was criticized by great jurists and advocates for my unconventional views and unjudicial unenglish (the love of the long word or odd mintage—I confess my guilt). But I was incorrigible. The style is the man and I survive.

Sincere appreciation from esteemed members of the Bench and the Bar did come in and exhilarate my morale, but 'conscience clear, never fear' luscently led me on without affection or ill will.

May I, in all humility, illustrate one short paragraph from the citation on the conferment of doctorate on me by the National Law School of India University:

> *It is difficult to comprehend in this brief citation the varied accomplishments of the man who gave Indian jurisprudence a people-oriented vision and put the judiciary in the centre-stage of constitutional politics. Suffice it to say that there is no Indian Judge till date, living or dead, on whom two (now three) doctoral theses have been written by scholars in two (now three) different Universities. Mr. Justice V.R. Krishna Iyer has that distinction. In honouring such a legal luminary and popular leader, the National Law School of India University is in fact reflecting the sentiments of admiration and respect of the entire legal community to a great judge and humanist this century has produced.*

I was greeted, when appointed, by a large number of 'hostile' lawyers writing a letter to the Times of India accusing me of being a dangerous man on the Bench. I kept my cool and my conscience. By the grace of God, those who came to 'scoff remained to 'pray'. Eventually suspicion died down. I had no enemies at the Bar, so far as I know, and my friends generally appreciated my stance, so I assume. I imparted a literary touch and adopted a new mode of writing judgments ignoring the traditional pattern. I tried to democratize judicial remedies and brought into vogue Public Interest Litigation and 'epistolary' jurisdiction—a letter complaining of injury being received as a *Us* Procedural lissomness and informality, in a poor country, is an aspect of access to Justice. I did pay my humble tribute to human rights by introducing the values of the International Covenants into Indian law by hermeneutic humanism. I tried, with some measure of success, to liberalise the prisons, to sensitize sentencing correctionally, to enliven liberties and to pragmatise gender justice and dalit equity. Life, the right to life, claimed my judicial reverence and so, life-saving parameters were given high priority judicial sanction by me, making capital punishment the rarest of the rare verdicts from the court. Imagine that great judge, Lord Scarman following my two anti-death sentence rulings in a Privy Council pronouncement and writing to me, a stranger, how moved he was by my passionate plea in *Eduga Annamma* and *Rajendra Prasad Singh.* PIL has become a phenomenal success and I am happy, although stray abuses of that process disturb my souL I strove to humanise conceptually the narrow *locus standi* notion, whereby the people had a larger chance of access to justice. This *open sesame* has come to stay. I have some satisfaction that labour jurisprudence has received enlarged jurisdiction through a few of my judgments. Social justice—read any of my judgments—claimed my heart and shaped my thought. I tried, with some success, to discipline that self-serving heritage of contempt jurisprudence.

Some of my colleagues, all of whom I respect, have been harsh on me and have differed from me. Why not? Law develops by diverse views and, in flashes of collision, unfold truth and justice. I have sought to sanctify my judgments at times by quoting Mahatma Gandhi and Swami Vivekananda, Dr. Ambedkar and Sri. Aurobindo and the Bible. My judicial vocabulary has been more vivid, than hackneyed, less voguish than dull, drab verbalism. My constituency has been the lowliest, the last and the lost as my judgments will substantiate. Both the proletariat and proprietariat matter equally, I have written a profusion of judgments, far more than those who had a comparably brief term of seven years. Off the Bench, I continue the same philosophy as governed me in court, in the field of criminal justice.

Perhaps, I have *failed* in the short run. Death sentence on death sentence is my living faith but a lost cause because my colleagues' conscience struck a ferocious note, true to their faith. But the United Nations Protocol is on my side. On prohibition, I was Gandhian and constitutionalist, writing, as I did, a long and learned opinion in support of effective 'dry days'. But when the history of the Judiciary comes to be written, the last word may not bring me tears.

If you ask me which was the most politically sensational case I decided I would say that the order on the Stay Petition in the election appeal filed by Smt. Indira Gandhi against the Allahabad High Court judgment, described by jurist Seervai as reaching the finest hour of the highest court. If you ask me which trend of jurisprudence I inaugurated happily I would say it was Public Interest Litigation and Epistolary Process and the *Ratlam Municipality* case. If you ask me which ruling solaced my soul most I would say it was those two decisions setting aside death sentences. Criminal jurisprudence fulfills its functional trust when life and liberty are saved for even the least of humanity.

Such is my life and its link with the rule of law, in brief.

EPILOGUE

I am four score and six, perhaps, perhaps a little more is left of the candle of life to burn. So, I *must* cease to be I but identify myself with *That,* to with all living creatures, the micro-self merging in the Universal Self. Meanwhile, my urgent aspiration at life's sunset is to transform the spiritual trust and temporal tryst with destiny, along the lines of Kipling:

If you can fill the unforgiving minute
With sixty seconds' worth of distance run,
Yours is the Earth and everything that's in it,
And—which is more—you'll be a Man, my son!
Where the mind is without fear and the
Head is held high;
Where knowledge is free;
Where the mind is led forward by thee into
Ever-widening thought and action—
Into that heaven of freedom, my Father,
Let my country awake. (Gitanjali)

Constitutional Socialism, Right to Life and Food Security Bill

The Indian Constitution takes note of the reality of poverty of the majority of both humanity and provides for the right to life on an egalitarian foundation. This right is fundamental and postulates dignity and decency beyond bare existence. Life can subsist in our material world only if nutritious food is available. Poverty is negation of nutritious food. Therefore, affordable quality and quantity of food to those who starve and are destitute is basic today. The reality is 42 crores are in below poverty line, 70% people's daily earning income is Rs. 20. In starvation India ranks first among 26 African countries suffering utter starvation.

Socialism is social justice and for a poor family it has meaning only if food is available in the market at an affordable price. The truth today is that starvation strikes if food security in the right to life is an obligation of the State is equally necessary to make the State socialist and democratic. Two million Indians go to sleep (?) on a hungry stomach. This situation is a constitutional mockery of the right to life. Long after we are independent and liberated from British imperialism the Indian Government has awakened to this gross disparity and so at long last it has decided to introduce a bill ensuring food security to the have not category which is nearly 70% of our population. It is in these circumstances that for the first time the Central Government has chosen to make food available to the entire human cycle. Pregnant women are the source of Indian population and they need nutritious food for the babe in the womb to survive and be born. So the bill provides the right of pregnant woman to get nutritious food. Nutritious food involves the quality and quantity of the food supply. The mother who lactates her to find good food to fulfill its obligations as mother and so require free food. If they are below the poverty line the bill takes care of food availability for these categories. A child is the special focus of the nation's future and the bill takes special notice of that factor. The student community is the backbone of the Government's strength and so the bill provides for and students get good food. Research for better technology in the production of food is taken care of by a Central pool and wherever necessary is provided so that the States may be assured of sure supply where it is short of the required quantity. In short starvation is nearly abolished when the bill goes into operation. India lives in its villages. Therefore food supplies must be the publicity of local governments so that distribution. The financial requirements for the bill to function are around 2000 crores, too heavy for a State to undertake. Therefore, federal Indian Constitution has made the Central Government bear the heavy responsibility.

For the first time the pragmatic meaning of socialism and democracy is taken serious note of. The Constitution mandates social and economic justice. The Directives have hardly been implemented in India with a few wealthy and a flood of illthy humanity steeped in dismal desperate downtrodden condition. In such a society silence is a far cry in Indian history. Starvation has been given a shock by the food security bill but law deals with life only if enforced effectively with popular cooperation. We are yet to see what Parliament prefers with their bill and whether the Executive implements to reach the last hungry child and old man in India with unemployment on the increase, terrorism springing up. Everywhere socialism is boloney only if the food security bill becomes a factor of life.

"Sathyameva Jayate"

Is the Little Socialist India Legally Yours? No. Look at the Rabid Pride of Petrol

The Preamble to the constitutional diction contradicts our democratic Republic is governed by the little man with a little mark on a little ballot collectively organized on plural party basis. The needy people of India can hardly afford even the existing petrol price which is a blow on the economy of the poor. Every fundamental right will suffer adversely by this measure. The cost of living, of travel and every dimension of life will suffer a shock by your audacious measure of magnifying fuel price by Rs. 7.54 since it is too high to be tolerated. I hope you will get your lesson in the next election when people in their indignant indigents and downtrodden condition will put you in your proper place for this reckless aggravation of oil price. You must think of other creative ways of reducing consumption of petrol and energy and not punish the poor for your bankruptcy of ideas. Tirunalveli District in Tamil Nadu has wind power. Creative research on solar energy, tidal power etc., much can be done. But if you dare not think beyond the conventional way of raising petrol price people most of whom are *Kuchelas* will retaliate in anger. It will be by then too late for you to learn the price of anti-people fuel price. Please reduce the petrol price at once if you want the little man of India to survive and the right to life respected.

With great regards to you Prime Minister whom I consider a Statesman why then have you malignantly done this cruel measure on the have-not humanity? You fancy you are infallible, No. You are infallible because of a flattering provision in the Constitution. The little man will overrule it if you wound him like this.

Diesel Price Hike – More Tears – Common Man

Are we democratic? No. The little Indian of Kerala is victim of high traffic prices. No movement, no domestic purchases, life becomes costly. Petrol is costly. So everyone turns to diesel. If diesel prices go up it is a blow on those below the poverty line. It is a case of no freedom of movement, no freedom of association, no free speech virtually no Fundamental Right. A State respects the Constitution cannot raise the prices of commodity without which movement of the poor is possible. About 70000 auto rickshaws ply on diesel. All those who have cars and automobiles use petrol. Those who belong to BPL are without auto rickshaws.

Dear Oommen Chandy, you resist this price rise of diesel which is a blow to the belly of the BPL. Democracy means more than the little ballot paper but every facility needed for going to the polling station and casting his vote and going back home for food, if any. All these are affected by raising Diesel prices. You have won by the ballot and if you are an honest democrat you must give those BPL people more facility and not make life costly for them. Don't betray your pledges. Today for cheaper cars you seek diesel engines for cheaper travel cost, you seek auto rickshaws. In this light every rupee more for diesel is a stab on the domestic budget of the BPL. In the next election this price rise will find the poor against you unless they are hoodwinged by propaganda or the Shavian cynicism is proved true. Did he not say: 'He who can does, he who cannot touches'. (Bernard Shaw)

I see vividly the domestic budget upset by diesel rise in price. The women cannot go shopping because the auto rickshaws will shoot up the rates. The gas supplies have been drastically reduced, so there will be a crisis in every kitchen. Today, less gas means less tea, less coffee, more angry husbands, more desperate wives and ill-treated children. This chaos will breed more violence at home and outside. Those who can see distant things can find in the offing more Naxalites, more Maoists ultimately a Government falls when terrorism spreads.

Dear Oommen Chandy, you travelled to the people, talked to them and gave access to them. Reduce the price of Diesel by internal economy and public taxation and putting pressure on the Centre. Kerala gone, Delhi too will be shaken out of office if we two matter better reverse the gear. No higher price for gas nor black-marketing but that is inevitable. Once you reduce supplies with a heartless hand. Why hasten your mortality when the Left is lost by infighting. Don't estrange the poor or hound the have-nots by the diesel price rise is a strategy for suicide which Rs. 5 more at a single brazen escalation. You are asking the have-nots to drive you out. Even now by your thoughtless plan-less performance you have the ignominy of topping child mortality in the world but a shame. The stratagem of monkeying with diesel prices is a psychic trick thinking that the poor man will not see through your double game. You are inviting the anger of the masses by playing with gas supplies and price hikes of diesel. If the Government calls it is the price of folly diesel and gas are tempting now. But the police and firing may be the option tomorrow and the day after. I am unhappy at this prospect but what is inevitable cannot be wished away. Dear Oommen Chandy, your politics and longevity will keep you a long way of prudence and genuine love if the weaker sector has your sympathy in taxation and public control.

The Buddha, Mahatma Gandhi Violence and Robbery—Universal Corrodes National Economy

The Indian economy is a colonial manifestation of British imperialism. Way back in 1498 came Vasco-de-Gama into Calicut who set foot on native soil and gradually occupied under the zamorin rule, then followed other European countries, Dutch, Portuguese, German and finally the British. The guns of the West under guise of trade and business proved a menace too powerful for the native weapons to resist. Eventually in a long story of battles and victory India became the largest Empire under the British Queen. The British Viceroy controlled by the British House of Commons became the ruler of India. India lost its independence and over 600 native Princess owed their loyalty to the British Queen in the Buckingham Palace. The finest civilization and cultural marvel were developed in India. Max Muller, the German Philosopher said this of India's pinnacle of culture:

If we were to look over the whole world to find out the country most richly endowed with all the wealth, power, and beauty that nature can bestow – in some parts a very paradise on earth – I should point to India. If I were asked under what sky the human mind has most fully developed some of its choicest gifts, has most deeply pondered over the greatest problems of life, and has found solutions of some of them which well deserve the attention even of those who have studied Plato and Kant – I should point to India. And if I were to ask myself from what literature we here in Europe, we who have been nurtured almost exclusively on the thoughts of Greeks and Romans, and of one Semitic race, the Jewish, may draw the corrective which is most wanted in order to make our inner life more perfect, more comprehensive, more universal, in fact more truly human a life, not for this life only, but a transfigured and eternal life – again I should point to India.

With all this glory the white man dominated and made India a colony. This cultural collapse did not last long. Indian National Congress sprang into existence in a struggle. Subash Chandra Bose, Jawaharlal Nehru, Mahatma Gandhi and thousands and thousands of Indians rose to Everest heights and thus dawned a national liberation movement all non-violent; the like of which history has not seen. Under the leadership of Gandhiji and the spiritual inspiration of Vivekananda this militant movement won its grand objective of independence. The Indian independence movement was ultimately gained by the House of Commons passing a liberation legislation making India a great Republic. In a historic speech on the 15th of August, 1947 the first Prime Minister of India Nehru proclaimed a tryst with destiny formally inaugurating a socialist, secular, democratic Republic of India. A free Constituent Assembly representing the voice of the Indian people sat and after prolonged debates drafted a great Constitution for India *i.e.* Bharat and on the 26th January, 1950 India became a glorious Republic Socialist Secular and Democratic. We are proud today of being the largest democracy in the world which is at once socialist, secular and democratic. The founding fathers of India through years of debate in the Constituent Assembly created perhaps the largest Constitution in the world promised the vast Indian people. Federal Court with several States under it based on the common people's ballot. The sovereign power that governs our nation today is based on the little man's vote although most Indian people are poor and the wealth is cornered by a majority of rich men. It is this blend of wealthy and illthy Indians who make up our nation under the Constitution. We are under the Preamble itself a socialist secular democratic Republic. The challenge of economy is to transform India into a socialist polity no longer theocratic but transcending all religions but united through a divinity that makes and unites spiritually the entire Indian people into one unity of divinity represented by the Father of the Nation Mahatma Gandhi.

The Buddha—His Bone and Soul

Lord Buddha was born in Lumbini, Nepal, as a world heritage site and birthplace of Gautama Buddha. There are also claims about birthplace of Gautama Buddha to be Kapileswara, Orissa or Kapilavastu at Piprahwa, Uttar Pradesh. He became a prince and a ruler. India was poor and Bihar abounded in misery and poverty. The suffering of people moved the Prince so much that he could not continue with his princely prosperity and decided to renounce his princedom. The word Buddha is a title for the first awakened being in our cosmic age. "Buddha" meaning "Awakened One" or the "Enlightened One". The date of his birth and death are uncertain. But historians hold divergent views between c.568 BCE to 483 BCE. Traditional biography attributes to him many miracles. But he himself was astonishingly secular and rational. His father King Suddhodana was the leader of Shakya clan whose capital was Kapilavastu at Uttar Pradesh. Siddhartha is said to have spent 29 years in Kapilavastu. He saw old men, sick people and suffering humanity. This shook him in his soul and he abandoned princely ostentation and courted a mendicant life. He begged and when King Bimbisara offered him his throne Siddhartha rejected it. Siddhartha and a group of five companions led by Kaundinya are then said to have set out to take their austerities even further. After nearly starving himself to death by restricting his food intake to around a leaf or nut per day, he collapsed in a river while bathing and almost drowned. The Buddha described Nirvana as the perfect peace of a mind that is free from ignorance, greed, hatred and other afflictive states. Nirvana according to the Buddha is liberation. He travelled for remaining 45 years of his life. Buddha is said to have traveled in the Gangetic Plain, in what is now Uttar Pradesh, Bihar and southern Nepal. He came into close contact with nobles, outcaste street sweepers and murderers. The Buddha was sought to be assassinated many times. But when they actually met him they gave up the idea. He died at the age of 80 and remains an inspiration of the highest sublime life ever thereafter. Of him, Swami Vivekananda said:

Let me tell you a few words about one man who actually carried this teaching of Karma-Yogi into practice. That man is Buddha. He is the one man who ever carried this into perfect practice. All the prophets in the world, except Buddha, had external motives to move them to unselfish action. The prophets of the world, with this single exception, may be divided into two sets, one set holding that they are incarnations of God come down to earth, and the other holding that they are only the messengers from God; and both draw their impetus for working from outside, however highly spiritual may be the language they use. But Buddha is the only prophet who said. "I do not care to know your various theories about God. What is the use of discussing all the subtle doctrines about the soul? Do good and be good. And this will take you to freedom and to whatever truth there is." He was, in the conduct of his life, absolutely without personal motives; and what man worked more than he? Show me in history one character who has soared so high above all. The whole human race has produced but one such character, such high philosophy, such wide sympathy, yet had the deepest sympathy for the lowest animals, and never put forth any claims for himself. He was the ideal Karma-Yogi, acting entirely without motive, and the history of humanity shows him to have been the greatest man ever born; beyond compare the greatest combination of heart and brain that ever existed, the greatest soul power that has ever been manifested. He was the first great reformer the world has seen. He was the first who dared to say, "Believe not because some old manuscripts are produced, believe not because it is your national belief, because you have been made to believe it from your childhood; but reason it all out, and after you have analysed it, then, if you find that it will do good to one and all, believe it, live up to it, and help others to live up to it." He works best who works without any motive, neither for money, nor for fame, nor for anything else; and when a man can do that, he will be a Buddha, and out of him will come the power to work in such a manner as will transform the world. This man represents the very highest ideal of Karma-Yogi.

The awakening of the Buddha synchronized with the realization of him of four foundational fundamental truths. Hindus claim the

Buddha to be an incarnation of Vishnu. The Bahais and Christians and the Muslims claimed him as prophet. In sum, the Buddha belonged to all religion but was universal as a prophet whose jurisdiction was the entire earth. The Buddha, who was an ascetic in life and died in sheer renunciation and his teachings were hostile to Brahminism. One of the greatest royal disciples of the Buddha was Ashoka. Of him, H.G. Wells the great historian in his Outline of History wrote:

> For eight-and-twenty years Asoka worked sanely for the real needs of men. Amidst the tens of thousands of names of monarchs that crowd the columns of history, their majesties and graciousnesses and serenities and royal highnesses and the like, the name of Asoka shines, and shines almost alone, a star. From the Volga to Japan his name is still honoured. China, Tibet, and even India, though it has left his doctrine, preserve the tradition of his greatness. More living men cherish the memory today than have ever heard the names of Constantine or Charlemagne.

The many religions we have amidst us do not elevate our spiritual unity but create Gods who rival with each other and did not promote that unity in divine dignity without which humanity has no future.

Beyond Deserts, rivers and seas of the Middle East the several civilization rose with Brahminical traditions and priest craft. He was a good-looking, capable young man of fortune, and until he was twenty-nine he lived the ordinary aristocratic life of his time. It was not a very satisfying life intellectually. There was no literature except the oral tradition of the Vedantic epics, and that was chiefly monopolized by the Brahmins; there was even less knowledge.

He was married at nineteen to a beautiful cousin. For some years they remained childless. He hunted and played and went about in his sunny world of gardens and groves and irrigated rice-fields. And it was amidst this life that a great discontent fell upon him. It was the unhappiness of a live brain that seeks fulfillment. He lived amidst plenty and beauty, he passed from gratification to gratification, and his soul was not satisfied. It was as if he heard the destinies of the race calling to him for higher development. He felt that the existence he was leading was not the reality of life, but a temporal holiday – a holiday that had gone on too long. When the mind grapples with a great and intricate problem of materialism, it makes its advances, it secures its splendid march step by step, but little realization of the gains it has made, until suddenly, with an effect of abrupt illumination, it realizes its victory. So it would seem it happened to Gautama. He had seated himself under a great tree by the side of a river to eat, when this sense of clear vision came to him. It seemed to him that he saw life plain. He is said to have sat all day and all night in profound thought, and then he rose up to impart his vision to the world. The fundamental teaching of Gautama, as it is now being made plain to us by the study of original sources, is clear and simple and in the closest harmony with modern ideas. It is beyond all disputes the achievement of one of the most penetrating intelligences the world has ever known.

Prince Buddha had many countries adopted his faith like Thailand, Cambodia, Myanmar, Bhutan, Sri Lanka, Tibet, Vietnam, Japan, Nagaland, China etc. Buddhism is a world religion and politically stood for world peace, abolition of poverty and slavery and was all for humanitarianism. Buddhism had a hold in the mind of Nehru who allowed Taiwan and recognized Dalai Lama to reside in India. Although it was not a State religion a considerable number of Indians had great faith in Buddhism. This great prince had only son Rahula but judging by the number of people whose mind was Buddhist he was a world wonder. Mahatma Gandhi was Buddhist in his highest ideals. It so happens that a man who was ascetic renounced material power and wealth remains the noblest soul ever alive. From the Buddha to Mahatma Gandhi is India's cultural heritage like Ramakrishna Paramahamsa and Vivekananda. Prince Buddha like a bright star in the sky and still remains a most powerful lustre who illumined generation after generation the heart and souls and the spiritual conviction of mankind. The great Buddha was a spiritual guru and sublime guide in the higher life of humanity. The best exposition of this supreme human being is what H.G. Wells has said of him. Read it, re-read it and let him transform you into a truly saintly selfless soul:

We have what are almost certainly the authentic heads of his discourse to the five disciples which embodies his essential doctrine. All the miseries and discontents of life he traces to insatiable selfishness. Suffering, he teaches, is due to the craving individuality, to the torment of greedy desire. Until a man has overcome every sort of personal craving his life is trouble and his end sorrow. There are three principal forms the craving of life takes, and all are evil. The first is the desire to gratify the senses, sensuousness. The second is the desire for personal immortality. The third is the desire for prosperity, worldliness. All these must be overcome that is to say, a man must no longer be living for himself before life can become serene. But when they are indeed overcome and no longer rule a man's life, when the first personal pronoun has vanished from his private thoughts, then he has reached the higher wisdom, Nirvana, serenity of soul. For Nirvana does not mean, as many people wrongly believe, extinction, but the extinction of the futile personal aims that necessarily make life base or pitiful or dreadful.

According to Sri Lankan legends, when the Lord Buddha died his tooth was retrieved from the funeral pyre and kept in a temple in Kandy, Sri Lanka. This historic personality passed away in 483 BCE and he died on the earth but lived on as star as immortal in the sky illumining humanity in spiritual splendour and moral wonder. The like of him if I may eulogize no eye had seen ever thereafter, no heart conceived and no tongue can adequately tell.

When the cultural odyssey comes to a written two great spirits will stand out as marvels, Gautama Buddha and Mahatma Gandhi. They are luminous wonders which illumine as spreading Nirvana and Poorna Swaraj.

Bapuji, the Father of the Indian Nation – An Eternal Tomorrow

Tomorrow is the 2nd of October, the birthday of the greatest man of our generation, Mahatma Gandhi. Ideologically Gandhiji made three fundamental principles as his basic creed – Non-co-operation with evil, Non-violence and Satyagraha. The spiritual quintessence of Indian culture were contained in these three principles and if this trinity of values were jettisoned India's high place in the comity of nations will no longer be respected but inside the country exploitation prevail because we were a colony under the British Empire. To overthrow this colonial stature the Indian National Congress Party was formed with a dominant Britisher A.O. Hume but the life blood of the Congress was to win back swaraj. The daring dazzling light of swaraj from the days when the Congress Party was formed by Gandhiji in 1888. He was the conscience of the Congress and dared to defy the imperial crown. He was described as a 'half-naked fakir' because he lived the life of a simple Indian half-naked, half-fed who would never bend before any emperor and was committed to truth without compromise. In this sense Gandhiji was fearless and as Bernard Shaw put it: 'It is dangerous to be too good.' In his career we had to offend the loss of British India. He suffered 2888 days in jail for the cause of his principles. He stood against castism and communalism and for him Hindus and Muslims were integral to humanity. He struggled and sacrificed his life for communal unity and died as he was shot and killed. As he died on earth his body perished but there arose a new star in the sky which stood for those eternal principles which made him the Father of the Indian Nation. Today he is a world figure and is the symbol of truth and non-violence. Bapuji was a lawyer by profession. The Mahatma as a lawyer was a great soul and in court whether for or against his client he would speak only the truth. So much so, the judges would simplicity accept what Gandhiji told them. Gandhi as a lawyer was a sublime figure. Unfortunately there was only one Gandhi who was so uncompromising in speaking the truth and truth alone and strove for a peaceful settlement on a just basis whether the settlement was for his client's benefit or not. Gandhiji's politics were his principles. He shaped the Congress Party during its moderate and extremist days. He was a barrister of an unusual client and would walk up to the throne with an erect spine. He is the Father of our Nation but remains mostly in statutes and quotations for he was too divine to be followed by ordinary humanity. Where he walked was hallowed ground, where he sat was shrine. Gandhiji was against death sentence and his criminology was for transformation of the good in man and elimination of the evil in him. To wipe every tear and share suffering from your brethren was his motto. His theory of penology was against retribution because he believed that an eye for an eye only ends up making the whole world blind.

'It is better to be violent, if there is violence in our hearts, than to put on the cloak of non-violence to cover impotence.'

Alas! Gandhi the Mahatma, the spiritual splendour is no longer extant. So India and the world have promises to keep and miles to go before they sleep if Bapuji is still our leader. The earth is the home of all humanity blended with divinity with two wonders keeping its civilization glorious and they are Lord Buddha, the Prince of Kapilavasthu and Mahatma Gandhi, the star who shone from Porbandar, Gujarat.

A Day of Wonder

Matha Amritanandamayi is a grand personality of Global greatness, a modern Rishi with Love for all Creation as her medium. In a World of corruption, terror and decline she is an *avatar* of celestial light and love committed to one cause, the unity of humanity and divinity through no magic nor riddle save compassion and embrace of affection. No Caste, no Creed, no Community, no Gods in rivalry. All Creation is a single Divinity. With this unity of vision and mission of egalite, no poverty, food for the hungry child, home for the homeless, a little plea of earth for the humblest – and free hospitalization for the sick and spiritual Joy above material pleasures. This is her mission. This is the invocation.

Mathrudevo Bhava!

Pithrudevo Bhava!

Acharyadevo Bhava!

Athidhidevo Bhava!

Daridradevo Bhava!

That is real Wealth. Amritapuri is the earth's capital where equality, no Poverty prevail Mata's Social Justice, Economic Justice and Political Justice. You Mataji are being celebrated the world over for your 59th birthday. You have no death. Long after your body is gone. You will spread love for all Humanity. Mathaji, you are truly a wonder of humanity and divinity blended to make this earth a hallowed planet. Where you sit is shrine, where you walk is hallowed ground. Your gentleness with which you received me in your 59th birthday is a moment whichever shines. I salute you on behalf of all mankind.

Kerala is ridden by castes, creeds, faiths and Gods together making social life full of chaos. Islam speaks of a single faith and a world of unity embracing all humanity. The world is one and there is only one God Allah and there is only one capital Mecca. But polygamy of the male sex is continued although for women monogamy is the rule. Islam is a major faith in India and in Kerala Christianity the other major religion of the world also believes in mankind as one. Single faith centering round Jesus Christ whose great faith is love. Buddhism is a sublime creed standing against violence and luxuries. The Buddha was a prince but he was a great humanist. Of him Vivekananda said:

Let me tell you a few words about one man who actually carried this teaching of Karma-Yogi into practice. That man is Buddha. He is the one man who ever carried this into perfect practice. All the prophets in the world, except Buddha, had external motives to move them to unselfish action. The prophets of the world, with this single exception, may be divided into two sets, one set holding that they are incarnations of God come down to earth, and the other holding that they are only the messengers from God; and both draw their impetus for working from outside, however highly spiritual maybe the language they use. But Buddha is the only prophet who said. "I do not care to know your various theories about God. What is the use of discussing all the subtle doctrines about the soul? Do good and be good. And this will take you to freedom and to whatever truth there is." He was, in the conduct of his life, absolutely without personal motives; and what man worked more than he? Show me in history one character who has soared so high above all. The whole human race has produced but one such character, such high philosophy, such wide sympathy, yet had the deepest sympathy for the lowest animals, and never put forth any claims for himself. He is the ideal Karma-Yogi, acting entirely without motive, and the history of humanity shows him to have been the greatest man ever born; beyond compare the greatest combination of heart and brain that ever existed, the greatest soul power that has ever been manifested. He is the first great reformer the world has seen. He was the first who dared to say, "Believe not because some old manuscripts are produced, believe not because it is your national belief, because you have been made to believe it from your childhood; but reason it all out, and after you have analysed it, then, if you find that it will do good to one and all, believe it, live up to it, and help others to live up to it." He works best who works without any motive, neither for money, nor for fame, nor for anything else; and when a man can do that, he will be a Buddha, and out of him will come the power to work in such a manner as will transform the world. This man represents the very highest ideal of Karma-Yogi.

In spite of all these religions Kerala society derived to the common man justice, social, economic and political. There was poverty and suffering. With the result that untouchability even unapproachability prevails and made social life wretched. So Gandhiji's message that true religion is against suffering of some and happiness should go and to wipe every tear from every eye was the Mahatma whose sublime supreme creed against violence, casteism and untouchability. He stood for human unity regardless of religion. But Kerala society remains lunatic and did not practice fraternity. It is in this context that Narayana Guru born from the lower caste Ezhava rose for higher religion and spirituality. He revolutionized Kerala theology and blended materialism and spiritualism. This great saintly leader stood for a higher philosophy of life but died by his sublime thought remained half finished. There arose a supreme leader from our women *advaita*, the gift of Adi Sankara. She stood alike for religious unity and fraternity. It is in her 59th birthday that lakhs of people gathered in her humble village near Quilon. Her glorious name Matha Amrithanandamayi was the gospel of love and donations poured in form various parts of the country particularly from the United States. With this abundance of charity Mathaji as she is popularly known started educational and medical institutions because elimination of poverty and suffering and unifications of all mankind was her goal. Her 59th birthday was celebrated at Amritapuri and lakhs of people attended the function. I too with several friends drove from Kochi to Amritapuri 360 miles. I drove up and down with my friends in three cars and had darshan of Mathaji. A whole day was spent dedicated for getting a darshan. She received me, blessed me and my friends. It was a great day, a day of illumination and of wonder. To meet and get a glimpse of a person belonging to the fisherman caste but taller than the tallest of contemporary Rishis was a day of wonder.

The Chandrasekharan Butchery – Terrorist Public Economy of Revolutionary Barbarity

Mahatma Gandhi stood for the politics of non-violence and peaceful political rivalry. But in his country India the other day a leader of a new party called the Revolutionary Marxist Party was hacked to pieces for reasons still under investigation. Political motivation being the broad mandate before the brutality which led to Chandrasekharan's murder with over 50 violent injuries on top of a bombing which initially maimed him. The criminal investigation is going on but behind it is the political motivation. Of course, India is primitive and economically under-developed. But for the first time Chandrasekharan, a Communist leader deserted his party and formed a new party and paid the price of being slaughtered brutally. Various reasons are put forward as the cause. One thing is certain, rival politics is the reason for the noxious delinquency. Be that as it may, democracy in its lunatic immaturity alone can account for this savagery. Darwin taught us that in the process of evolution the human being emerged from its ancestor the monkey. Man himself in his collectivity adopted various social systems particularly capitalism and communism. The richer classes who formed the minority but owned the wealth of the nation became the haves who cornered economic power. They form the wealthy. The vast majority being poor were downtrodden and had become the proletariat who constituted the vast illthy. Inevitably there was a class conflict and a human *via*-media was the only pragmatic solution during our time. In these circumstances of tension and terrorism violence was inevitable and cultural decency and humanism a casualty. Survival of democracy in such savage environs was possible only by adopting the values enunciated in the grand Preamble of the Indian Constitution which I set out here:

"WE, THE PEOPLE OF INDIA, having solemnly resolved to constitute India into a SOVEREIGN SOCIALIST SECULAR DEMOCRATIC REPUBLIC and to secure to all its citizens:

JUSTICE, social, economic and political;

of thought, expression, belief, faith and worship;

EQUALITY of status and of opportunity;

and to promote among them all

FRATERNITY assuring the dignity of the individual and the unity and integrity of the Nation;

IN OUR CONSTITUENT ASSEMBLY this twenty-sixth day of November, 1949, DO HEREBY ADOPT, ENACT AND GIVE TO OURSELVES THIS CONSTITUTION."

This Preamble reads sublime in print but in practice it is seen to be hollow as best illustrated in the Chandrasekharan's savage murder, whoever may be guilty of this murder. There is a deep political delinquency. A shocking lunacy which has to be unearthed and new lessons in humanism must be manifested and journey from humanity to divinity has to take hold of the rule of law. Our judges instead of confining themselves to mere law and jurisprudence must rise to sublime heights and adopt a spiritual vision and transform society from the monopoly of the proprietariat to the democracy of the proliterate. This transformation is the only resolution of the ghastly Chandrasekharan tragedy. But what is taking place is vast verbal accusation between the Communist Party and the ideological battle remain unresolved. Leaders of all political parties who are patriotic enough to abide by swaraj is the necessity of the hour. Not a matter of Kerala and Tamil Nadu but involving the Indian people as a whole from Kashmir to Kanyakumari we must have one India, one people, a dynamic thesis of advaita. This new vision must be the product of the malignant Chandrasekharan gory event. Let the nation meet. Let the Legislators of the country hold a fruitful gathering. Let the judges of the country and the advocate as an Indian profession gather together. Meet debate and bring about a dialectical unity. Out of this chaos that prevails now a divine humane Preamble to our destiny must be fashioned. Such a democracy will be the beginning of a great Bharat, which will answer the splendid rhetoric eloquently expressed by the first Prime Minister of India who articulated the meaning of swaraj giving expression to the great truth of dearest value to the Father of the Nation. Here is what Nehru then orated:

> "Long years ago we made a tryst with destiny and now the time comes when we shall redeem our pledge not wholly or in full measure but very substantially. The service of India means the service of the millions who suffer, it means the ending of poverty and ignorance and disease and inequality of opportunity. The ambition of the greatest man of our generation has been to wipe every tear from every eye. That may be beyond us but as long as there are tears and sufferings, so long our work will not be over."

At this glorious hour I salute you all the representatives of the people of Bharat and appeal to you to live up to the grand heritage you have as your legacy. You do not represent your little constituency but the entire Indian people as great as the Ganga and the Himalayas. After all, India belongs not to the outdated princess but the democracy which represents 'the little man, walking into a little booth, with a little pencil, making a little cross on a little bit of paper – no amount of rhetoric or voluminous discussion can possibly diminish the overwhelming importance of the point'.

MANISHADA

A youngster namely T.P. Chandrasekharan, leader of the revolutionary Marxist Party is brutally murdered. It is shocking to note that 50 violent injuries on his top of a bombing which killed him.

The political parties, especially those who plead human rights and Marxism should be shocked at the incident. Ideology can't be fought with bomb or sword. If anybody thinks that by man slaughtering ideas can be finished, then there would have been no Christianity, Gandhism and even Marxism.

State, even when a citizen says no to its shelter is obliged to a void, criminal brutality since such acts offends peace, democracy and progress. State failed to protect law and order resulted in the death of this precious son of Kerala. I request Kerala Government to adopt scientific investigation to bring the culprits to law. I also expect that State will provide urgent financial assistance to the family of the late Chandrasekharan.

The Cultural Collapse of Kerala

He Prayeth Best, Who Loveth Best, All Things Great and Small

Read the countless dailies of Kerala media and you will see violence writ large sex inside families. Alcoholism in young and old and suicides growing in number; schools and colleges, hospitals and public offices sinking with corruption.

We are celebrating Onam. By accident it coincides with Ramzan. Allah, the Merciful stands for world brotherhood, cosmic fraternity and divinity by practicing humanity. No Muslim is a true Muslim unless he shares his wealth with brothers and sisters. So too no Buddhist is a true disciple of the Prince Buddha unless his heart shares the suffering of the poorest. The great religion of Hinduism through this Upanishads and *advaita* tells us the same lesson of practicing compassion, sharing not preaching. This realization of global agony is true religion. In short, be your religion what it may, you are truly pious only when you see in yourself your neighbour's vicissitudes. This was the great teaching of Vivekananda who in an address to high class Hindu in Madras feelingly observed:

Aye, Brahmins, if the Brahmin has more aptitude for learning on the ground of heredity than the Pariah, Give to the weak, for them all the gift is needed. Our poor people, these downtrodden masses of India, therefore, require to hear and to know what they really are. Aye, let every man and woman and child, without respect of caste or birth, weakness and strength, hear and learn that behind the strong and the weak, behind the high and the low, behind everyone, there is that Infinite Soul, assuring that infinite possibility and the infinite capacity of all to become great and good. Let us proclaim to every soul – 'Arise, awake and stop not till the goal is reached.'

This sublime fraternity is what we learnt from the Buddha not to worship on his bones, teeth, his hair as we now do by building temples for them and lose the cosmic comity and divinity which latent in that supreme soul who made a Prince gave up everything and beheld in humanity the unity of Creation. Of him Vivekananda said:

Let me tell you a few words about one man who actually carried this teaching of Karma-Yogi into practice. That man is Buddha. He is the one man who ever carried this into perfect practice. All the prophets in the world, except Buddha, had external motives to move them to unselfish action. The prophets of the world, with this single exception, may be divided into two sets, one set holding that they are incarnations of God come down to earth, and the other holding that they are only the messengers from God; and both draw their impetus for working from outside, however highly spiritual maybe the language they use. But Buddha is the only prophet who said. "I do not care to know your various theories about God. What is the use of discussing all the subtle doctrines about the soul? Do good and be good. And this will take you to freedom and to whatever truth there is." He was, in the conduct of his life, absolutely without personal motives; and what man worked more than he? Show me in history one character who has soared so high above all. The whole human race has produced but one such character, such high philosophy, such wide sympathy, yet had the deepest sympathy for the lowest animals, and never put forth any claims for himself. He is the ideal Karma-Yogi, acting entirely without motive, and the history of humanity shows him to have been the greatest man ever born; beyond compare the greatest combination of heart and brain that ever existed, the greatest soul power that has ever been manifested. He is the first great reformer the world has seen. He was the first who dared to say, "Believe not because some old manuscripts are produced, believe not because it is your national belief, because you have been made to believe it from your childhood; but reason it all out, and after you have analysed it, then, if you find that it will do good to one and all, believe it, live up to it, and help others to live up to it." He works best who works without any motive, neither for money, nor for fame, nor for anything else; and when a man can do that, he will be a Buddha, and out of him will come the power to work in such a manner as will transform the world. This man represents the very highest ideal of Karma-Yogi.

A true humanist is a Gandhian. A true Gandhi disciple is a Buddhist. The world of Buddha is the world of Jesus Christ who commanded us to love our neighbor, why our enemies too? Islam is well-being of everyone. He who cannot contain in his bosom the entire wonder of creation is no Muslim. Fanaticism, terrorism and hatred of all religions other than ones own is not Muslim. He is a leader. Today, we see all humanity as equal, poor or rich, sharing the wealth of the all and wiping the tears of everyone else. It is this fundamental duty of compassion towards all living creatures that the great religion has proclaimed. This is read in the Indian Constitution as a fundamental duty and plead with mankind and Statesman everywhere to live in their generosity or fraternity of identity of humanity which is truly socialist, secularist and democratic.

"He Prayeth best, who loveth best; All things great and small; For the dear God who loveth us; He made and loveth all."

Mullaperiyar Controversy
A New Dynamic Pragmatic Solution

The Mullaperiyar Dam controversy is making bitterness between the people of Tamil Nadu, the people of Kerala and the two Governments loose their good relation over the dam controversy and its safety what with earth tremors and estrangement on the safety of water level of the Dam. The two Governments disagree on major issues. The water level Kerala wants to be 120 feet while Tamil Nadu wants 142 or thereabouts. Kerala demands reconstruction of a new Dam. A proposal fiercely opposed by Tamil Nadu and the Central Government has taken no active steps to negotiate between the two States on the two points to arrive at a reasonable happy resolution. The two peoples are driven to hate each other and this makes the federal relationship unhappy. In this context a happy proposal has been put forward by Kochouseph Chittilappilly with the active assistance and directions from two renowned structural engineering consultants. The cost according to their proposal will be around 55 crores as against 1000 crores involved in the construction of a new dam. Let engineers from both States examine this welcome proposal and if feasible accept it as a solution for the diehard controversy over Mullaperiyar Dam. The proponents of the new scheme had themselves offered without condition of a sum of Rs. 5.5 crores. I feel strongly that this excellent proposal credibly on the face of it and a boon facilitating a just resolution should be given a try by the two Governments. I hope public opinion in the two States will support this project and see an end of the hatred syndrome which aggravates the estrangement with everyday's delay. I appeal to the two Governments and the Central Government to consider this excellent creative proposal from a technical angle and if pragmatic and realistic burry-hatchet, re-establish cordial relation and go ahead with the Kochouseph Chittilappily's project.

A Posthumous Tribute to Kelu Nambiar

A great jurist has to be fearless, independent and erudite. Kelu was all these three. An obsequious jurist is a dangerous coward, a submissive law man and one who sells opinions for the sake of position and promotion. Kelu was a brave fighter, too bold to bend before the Bench. His use of the English language was powerful I cannot forgive his strong critics or my English – he was excellent but I liked his English without fear or favour, sharp diction never soft but always free from malignancy. He had a point always, an original jurisprudence. He was brief but longer in meaning than verbal essays, rarely cared for pleasing judges but his argument contained something new. Kelu was Kerala's incorruptible law teacher at the Bar who never stooped to conquer with his creative soul.

When I declare Kelu Nambiar was a jurisprudent I comprehend in that expression social engineering. Jurisprudence is the science of law designed to produce order in society. Sans law what prevails is chaos. The rule of law is therefore geared to produce peaceful conditions in the rule of life. No law, no order and jurists themselves should be orderly so that the courts of law use their writ power to see that everything society does or authorities perform is according to propitious promotive of friendship fraternity and homogeneity. This is possible only if those instrumentalities enforcing the rule of law like the Executive and Judicature possess integrity beyond purchase for money or partiality. If you seek a role model for these great virtues unerringly you reach one brave soul is Kelu Nambiar. He has criticized me and my English he has never bent before the robes on the Bench because his only purpose is not fee or victory but social order without affection or ill-will, fear or favour. Arbitrariness and bravado are his allergy. Kelu Nambiar will remain a model for the younger generation of the Bar for long.

V.S. Quits and Marxists in the Grip of a Split Syndrome

We are governed by a great Constitution adopted unanimously after long debate after the wisest exchange of ideological thought on social justice and cultural heritage. As finally approved India remains a socialist secular democratic Republic; several amendments have been made, plural parties have come in existence but at the end of 60 years India remains a socialist Republic with plural parties and multiple politics. For long India was an Empire under the British and had a federal trinity as in Briton. The Indian Legislature at the centre and in every State has rival parties. The one with the majority and which commanded the confidence of the Legislature forms the Government and rules the State or the country.

The opposition is made up of a plurality of parties, the largest among them being the Communist Party of India (Marxist). Mr. V.S. Achuthanandan representing the Marxist party is the Leader of the Opposition in the State Assembly. The party which is the Leader of the Opposition in a manner of speaking is Communist Party of India (Marxist) whose Secretary is Mr. Pinarayi Vijayan. Although the unity of the Communist Party (Marxist) is an inviolable factor, there is a crypto-division. Two groups emerged covertly, one headed by V.S Achuthanandan, a daring Communist but the party is headed by Pinarayi Vijayan, an outstanding Communist leader. An unfortunate rivalry of two personality cult developed in practice. Their disagreement to some extent weakened the Opposition. There were other smaller parties with individuality like the RSP and other tiny Leftist groups. India is democratic with the President and the Governor at the top of the Executive who are the Country or the State, elected by Parliament and obligated to act on the advice of the Cabinet who are answerable to the Parliament or the Assembly. All State power is accountable to the people through the Legislative

Houses. The Legislative Houses itself are accountable to the people and that is why periodic elections are an obligation in democracy. General elections are fundamental and the adult franchise makes it possible for the little man to make a mark on his little vote on a little piece of paper or by some other connivance. In short, the voice of any person matters. When the Leader of the Opposition vacates his office the Legislative Assembly fades as an authority attenuating the House as the voice of the people as a whole. If the Opposition is weak the party in power becomes authoritarian. As the implication of VS resigning is more than an MLA vacating his office but whittling down the entire democratic system and tending to promote fascism. In our system VS plays a powerful role in making the democratic system vigilant and critical of Government. When it misuses power and when this happens to divide the Opposition as a party, the casualty is democracy itself. That is why I insist that VS should not run away from his position. That endangers democracy. That shall not be and in this case VS is a tough person who will never surrender his conscience. The integrity of the great Legislative House as an institution is in peril when it becomes lame by VS walking out. To withdraw or run away is an act of cowardice. Fight. Not for the sake of power but for the people to express their will against wise. When a no confidence motion was moved against the Winston Churchill government during World War-II and British forces were receding when Hitler's planes were bombing in Briton and British survival as a power in Europe was at grave risk, Churchill used war words which should inspire every Opposition leader in a democracy facing a crisis of collapse. The spirit in which every Opposition leader including VS should act and should be inspired by Churchillian words. Be brave. You fight for a cause. That cause is the socialist integrity of Kerala and eventually India. VS, don't be a small man. Your spirit is straight and great so long as you are committed to inviolable socialism and truth. Let me conclude with those words of Churchill and apply it, adapting it to every force that socialist swaraj will become weak. No bomb, no murder, no propaganda will make you weak so long as you are honestly voicing the invincible socialism of our Constitution. Here is Churchill:

> We shall fight on the seas and oceans, we shall fight with growing confidence and growing strength in the air, we shall defend our island, whatever the cost may be, we shall fight on the beaches, we shall fight on the landing grounds, we shall

> fight in the fields and in the streets, we shall fight in the hills; we shall never surrender.

Dear Pinarayi, you are a great leader of Leftist Marxist. Don't wish away the Opposition. The Marxist Party in the current capitalist milieu and American colonial pressure needs a united and strong socialist Opposition. VS and you if united in resistance to the capitalist might our socialism has a chance. Together you must stand for the nation's sake, for the people's sake, we will win and make India a socialist democracy.

2012 Birthday Speech

Friends and Comrades

Today, the 15th November, 2012 is coming to a close. I bid good bye to 97 years of my earthily existence and march into my 98th year on this planet the sunset as it draws the curtain on daylight but in the twilight hours of dim darkness countless stars in the sky summon me to a difficult dubious world of withdrawal from ambition and achievements and entry into an age of humanity and divinity a new blend of life and beyond. It is in this mood of twilit vision that I sit here doubtful of my Tomorrow. But my country Bharat has a great culture of Vedic vintage of material and spiritual past which fills my mind with a mission of patriotic pride. With this bizarre background I wish all the inhabitants of our terrestrial space a rare mix of sombre and sublime happiness. Let the poor, the downtrodden and the have-nots be elevated to a level of egalitarian joy and elan of fraternity and homogeneity and brotherhood. In this pensive perspective, I look back to my long odyssey of life. I behold many appointments and disappointment, epic events and creative accidents. I see the childhood days of agrarian environs, my college days of thrill and great experiences as Minister, Legislator and Judge, what unfolds vividly before my memory is that verse from Robert Frost.

The woods are lovely, dark, and deep,

But I have promises to keep,

And miles to go before I sleep

And miles to go before I sleep

The woods are lovely dark and deep but I have promises to keep and yards (not miles) to go before I sleep and a mystery after death and my infinite sleep we call death. During the brevity of life of days, years or more I have expectations which may darken into anxiety, anxiety into dread and dread into despair. For a moment, I looked at the dais Chief Justice presiding and the Law Minister (Central) wanting to deliver his inaugural address and I a little Indian in the grip of old age with eyes and ears and legs weak with infirmities I thought of my colourful past and over 30 years of retired life busy with public activities living on pension alone. What next? That silence we know not what. I was in gloom. My mind was working. I want to go. Where? What is that world after death? I give up all I have to the Lord. He will take care of me. Tagore came to my mind. I traced the song which runs thus:

On the day when death will knock at thy door what wilt thou offer to him?

Oh, I will set before my guest the full vessel of my life—I will never let him go with empty hands.

All the sweet vintage of all my autumn days and summer nights,

All the earnings and gleanings of my busy life will I place before

Him at the close of my days when death will knock at my door.

Yes, Gitanjali was my pet poem I quoted in the battle of the Legislative Assembly debates which many members of the House did not understand nor my fellow activists at the Bar or on the Bench did.

The song that I came to sing remains unsung to this day.

I have spent my days in stringing and in unstringing my instrument.

The time has not come true, the words have not been rightly set; only there is the agony of wishing in my heart.—Tagore

Now that I am gone it is all empty. No, there is an after life. You can see and hear and live in a subtle world. That song is great if we care to.

Since I am appreciating a century of age somewhat unusual in our country my thoughts turn on Death De Profundis and you will forgive me to have robed your time away from life into the mystery of mortality. But as I opened my eyes again I see in each of you the presence of God. We don't have to look up the sky or the stars to see the God, the infinite. He is there in you, in me, in all creation. He sleeps in the insect, wakes in the vegetable, walks in the animal and thinks in man. Brilliant thinkers see beyond death and in this sense life is immortal. I have written a book on death and after where I have demonstrated that there are mediums, Raudive voices and many things which are imperishable. But speeches must stop somewhere and I do it here even as we part company when the meeting is dissolved. I must express my profound thanks to those who have organized this mysterious meet which is wrapped in a riddle inside an enigma.

I salute you all for having come and graced this function. I pray for the happiness to all human beings whether we believe in God or not we are real. My last words at this meeting is a prayer:

> "He Prayeth best, who loveth best; All things great and small; For the dear God who loveth us; He made and loveth all."

—Samuel Taylor Coleridge

Inaugural Address of Hon'ble Vice-President of India, Shri Hamid Ansari on the Occasion of the 97th Birthday of Shri Justice V.R. Krishna Iyer

I was commanded by the Legend to be here today and little choice did I have but to comply!

I candidly admit that I am happy and truly privileged to participate in today's function to celebrate the 97th birthday of Justice V.R. Krishna Iyer. "Sublimely mild, a spirit without a spot" is what can be said of Vaidyanathapura Ramakrishna Iyer, a man who made it his life's mission to resist injustice, secure justice and take up just and compassionate causes – within the realm of law and beyond it. Few would know of his passion for animal welfare or his early career in politics as a member of the Legislative Assembly.

It was indeed fortuitous that Justice Iyer came back to the Bar. He was a visionary in championing human rights jurisprudence with a focus on women, dalits and the marginalized, much before it emerged on the international or national scene. The vision and morality of our Constitution was his guide all through. His stint in the High Court and the Law Commission was focused on delivery of justice to the common citizen.

In a span of seven years as a Judge of the Supreme Court during 1973-1980, when the nation was in a political and legal tumult, Justice Iyer put the citizens and the values of the Constitution at the centre of his focus. The guarantees given to us by our founding fathers through the Constitution were reinterpreted for a new age, and new instruments fashioned to deliver justice. Thus, judicial remedies were sought through the instrumentalities of Public Interest Litigation, broader concepts of *locus standi*, and the Constitution was seen for what it could deliver to people.

His activism continued after retirement with renewed vigour, and is visible to this day. Justice Krishna Iyer can justifiably lay claim to be a Karma-Yogi all his life. In an opinion piece on 'justice, justices and justicing' a few years back, he made some pithy observations. Allow me to cite one of these:

> "There are three great pathologies that alienate the Judiciary from the people. The curative pharmacopoeia of fundamental judicial reform to counter these comprises forensic democratization, a process of social justice delivery and structural transformation of the judicial system through innovative facilities for the have-not humanity. This trinity of recipes demands institutional creativity, procedural humanism, and joint action by the Executive, the Legislature and the Judiciary, inspired by the radical values inscribed in the Constitution".

Prof. Upendra Baxi has rightly observed that Justice Iyer is "an embodiment of secular saintliness". He deserves the nation's appreciation and gratitude for his contribution. Ladies and Gentlemen,

Change, great change, has characterized the decades since Independence. The past two decades have accentuated the trend. The success of our polity is to be measured by the dexterity with which we have negotiated the rapids of this transformation.

As we survey the recent past, we notice a fundamental shift in the debate from development of economy and industry to human development. This has propelld the discourse with greater vigour to questions of sustainability and equity, to the quest for fairness and social justice, and for ensuring the right of every citizen to have equal access to opportunities for personal growth and development of one's capacities to the fullest, and for leading, fulfilling and meaningful lives. There is also recognition that there can be no sustainable improvement in public welfare without good and institutionalized processes of governance and unflinching commitment to democratic norms, constitutionally-anchored fundamental rights and universally-accepted human rights. At the global level over the past few decades a state of gross prosperity has been achieved; it remains unprecedented when looked at as an aggregate. The advances in terms of scientific and technological knowledge and applications far outstrip the combined achievement of humanity to date. We have produced ever more, consumed ever more, and wasted ever more than in history. Yet, we also know that these are aggregates, and averages always hide the condition of those below the average.

All over the world one hears today the cry of the common man protesting against the exclusion of the majority from accessing the benefits of economic growth and prosperity engendered by globalization of financial markets, economies, investment flows and processes. Real incomes of the top percentile across developed and emerging countries have grown disproportionately higher, exacerbating income inequalities. It is now clear that the system that has worked so well for the top percentile has delivered far lesser returns to others.

It is even more surprising that income distribution has worsened despite the great strides in narrowing the gaps in health and educational achievement across population groups. It is now globally recognized that human development is adversely affected under conditions of inequality, and that this can be quantified across indicators of health, education and income. Friends,

The Human Development Report, 2011 of the UNDP published last week has demonstrated that around a quarter of the human development at the global level is lost due to inequality. The South Asian region suffers the second largest human development losses due to inequality, after sub-Saharan Africa. In the case of India, there is an overall human development loss of over 28 per cent. due to inequality. The loss due to inequality of human development achievements in education are the highest in the case of India and amount to over 40 per cent. While the Report does not cover overlapping inequalities, we know from our experience that certain groups of marginalized such as women, scheduled castes and scheduled tribes, linguistic and religious minorities and those below the poverty line, experience multiple deprivations and exclusions.

Inequality is a problem in the long run, especially when it kills aspiration for personal and societal betterment. In India, the matrix of inequality spans gender, the rural-urban divide, class, caste, tribe, linguistic and cultural groups. While growth is a necessary condition for societal welfare, it is not sufficient and does not automatically lead to equality in accessing development and opportunities for growth.

Indeed, securing to all citizens equality of status and opportunity is a solemn resolve that finds mention in the Preamble of our Constitution. The State has a constitutional and moral duty to expand opportunities for those being left behind. Thus, the State has on the one hand focused on affirmative action and provision of a social safety net for those marginalized, while on the other moved to improving the capabilities of citizens to be more productive through skills and improved infrastructure.

Here, once again, I find of relevance what Justice Krishna Iyer has written:

> "If Indian democracy is to redeem its tryst with destiny, a creative protocol and code of ethics must become the vogue in public life. Consensus must be the rule of life, contentment of the lowliest the testament and participative process the habit of governance."

Ladies and Gentlemen,

As I conclude, I am reminded of the words of Dr. Rajendra Prasad on his election as the first President of independent India. "I have always held that the time for congratulation", he remarked, "is not when a man is appointed to an office, but when he retires".

I feel honoured to take part in the birthday celebrations of Justice Krishna Iyer and, in all humility, congratulate him for all his multifarious contributions to the nation, in and out of office.

Communalism, Godist Pluralism, Corruption and Colonialism

India that is Bharat is a land of the finest culture. Perhaps the most glorious in the world by authority is Max Muller the great German Philosopher who said a priceless passage:

> *If we were to look over the whole world to find out the country most richly endowed with all the wealth, power, and beauty that nature can bestow—in some parts a very paradise on earth—I should point to India. If I were asked under what sky the human mind has most fully developed some of its choicest gifts, has most deeply pondered over the greatest problems of life, and has found solutions of some of them which well deserve the attention even of those who have studied Plato and Kant—I should point to India. And If I were to ask myself from what literature we here in Europe, we who have been nurtured almost exclusively on the thoughts of Greeks and Romans, and of one Semitic race, the Jewish, may draw the corrective which is most wanted in order to make our inner life more perfect, more comprehensive, more universal, in fact more truly human a life, not for this life only, but a transfigured and eternal life—again I should point to India.*

Hinduism which is the faith of the people of Asia of Aryan origin and lofty theology prevailed all over India. There were over 600 Princess whose faith could be traced to the Vedas the epics of Ramayana and the sublime expression in the Bhagawat Gita. It is this culture whose quintessence was the soul of Mahabharata. Its ethos was so tolerant that when the Muslims extend India they had peaceful access and settled down to flourish as a religion. The great Eastern culture became universal and its splendour personified in the Buddha stood for unity of humanity and blended materialism with divinity. In this sense Hinduism was no religion but a brilliant combination of faith universal in character and omniscient in its tolerance. Hinduism is the world's third largest religion. Neither Islam nor Christianity was alien and so we could find in Indian temples, mosques and churches flourishing in close neighbourhood and in comity with each other. In short India basically was secular and its values were egalitarian. In this sense the Hindu faith was socialist. In believed in the Atman or the spiritual essence of everyone the greatest teachers asserted that there was God the Supreme Being in everyone and this enlightenment made the Bible and the Koran sacred texts with the Bhagawat Gita. This fundamental identity made India the home of theological pluralism in a dynamic unity. This cosmic comity is the ethos of Bharat. Aham Brahmasmi.

Who am I, asked the Hindu Philosopher Ramana Maharshi? It is this profound question and answer that every disciple learnt from him the kernel of Hinduism that remains the immortal imperishable Truth. Territorywise Hindus are substantially inhabitants of India, Nepal Bangladesh and Bali. Faith-wise Hindus are a heap of traditions upon tradition with no uniformity. There are a numberless God, plural sects. Many superstitions and castes come under Hinduism although they are rejected by reformers who claim the higher values of universality supramentalism as true Hinduism for a fuller understanding and the purity of Hinduism one has to confine oneself to Buddhism, teachings of Vivekananda, Ramakrishna Paramahamsa, Sree Narayana Guru, Adi Sankara, Ramana Maharshi and a host of other pioneers. Hinduism is not a religion but a way of life. Populationwise Hindus are over 1000 million and 4000 BC old. Hinduism is a cultural world of its own and Sanskrit is its original language although linguistic pluralism is part of Hinduism. Hinduism became a separate religion largely because of British imperialism and gulf Islamism with their aggressive control over India's resources. The best way to define this religion is to adopt the definition judicially rendered by the great Gajendragatkar who said:

> *"When we think of the Hindu religion, unlike other religions in the world, the Hindu religion does not claim any one prophet; it does not worship any one god; it does not subscribe to any one dogma; it does not believe in any one philosophic concept; it does not follow any one set of religious rites or performances; in fact, it does not appear to satisfy the narrow traditional features of any religion or creed. It may broadly be described as a way of life and nothing more."*

To end the thesis on Hinduism one asks the primary question Who am I? The answer to which tells us in a language of Ramana Maharshi what the soul of Hinduism is:

> *'Who am I?' I am not this physical body, nor am I the five organs of sense perception; I am not the five organs of external activity, nor am I the five vital forces, nor am I even the thinking mind. Neither am I that unconscious state of nescience which retains merely the subtle vasanas (latencies of the mind), while being free from the functional activity of the sense-organs and of the mind, and being unaware of the existence of the objects of sense-perception."*

Communalism in India has virtually divided the country between Hindus and Muslims. Although during the Second World War Hindus and Muslims making up the Indian Army and battled and sacrificed their lives for the sake of India swaraj. There was absolute unity between the two Communities. Later under Mahatma Gandhi they stood for unbreakable unity although the two communities were parting ways until at last there was a great partition signed in Simla and carried out with a greatest bleeding between two peoples notably the greatest mention.

•••